# HIGHWAY PATROL LOCATIONS THEN AND NOW

Broderick Crawford as Chief Dan Matthews

# HIGHWAY PATROL LOCATIONS THEN AND NOW

by Jerry L. Schneider

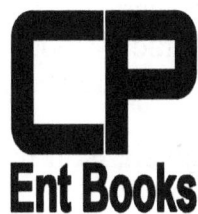

CP
Ent Books

**A CP Entertainment Books**
**First Edition**
**September 2014**


**Published by**
**Jerry Schneider Enterprises LLC**
**Victorville CA**
**e-mail: corriganvillepress@yahoo.com**

For a list of our books, please visit our web site at
**www.cpentbooks.com**




isbn: 978-0-9993672-2-3 (softcover)

# ACKNOWLEDGEMENTS

While the vast majority of this book is original research performed by the author, I would be remiss if I did not acknowledge the assistance of the following people in providing location help:

Marc Wanamaker of Bison Archives—Pacific Electric Sherman Yard, West Los Angeles
John Bengtson, Silent Echoes—Pacific Electric Sherman Yard, West Los Angeles
Gary Goltz—*Highway Patrol* website: http://www.highwaypatroltv.com
"thxdave" (identity unknown)—Various sites seen in Highway Patrol TV series in Google Maps

While the latter two persons and their websites have incorrect information in them, they also have a lot of good data—and Gary Goltz's site is a wonderful tribute to *Highway Patrol*.

\*   \*   \*   \*   \*

The entire series run of *Highway Patrol* is available on dvd from MGM/UA and TGG Direct, LLC. Unfortunately, it appears that the source material used for the transfer to digital format was video tape and not original 35mm and/or 16mm dupe prints/negatives. Because of the low quality of the transfer, it made my job of discovering the locations that much harder as street signs and signs on buildings were not crystal clear. But, those dvd's are the best available and are highly recommended.

# Table of Contents

# INTRODUCTION

The pilot for *Highway Patrol* was filmed April 11 to 13, 1955 by ZIV Television Programs, Inc. Since all of ZIV's television shows, at that time, were syndicated, until enough stations around the country decided to carry the show, it would not go into production. Into production it did go on August 22, 1955. The show premiered on October 3, 1955.

The show lasted for four seasons of 39 episodes per season for a total of 156 shows. Each show was usually filmed in 2 days—one day on location and one day in the studio. Occasionally, an additional day was necessary—usually because of helicopter usage in the episode. During season 1, ten of the thirty-nine episodes required three days of shooting.

The vast majority of the location work was done in Los Angeles County, a few episodes in Ventura County. Locations used in the first season varied widely, especially during the period in which the California Highway Patrol gave its complete support for the show. When that support was stopped and only an on-set technical adviser of the CHP (Officer Frank Runyon and Sergeant Mark Benson) was there, location work became more centralized, mostly in the San Fernando Valley and areas near the ZIV Studio in West Hollywood.

Some of the locations were very easy to locate as I either used to live near them or have visited them in my research on other locations. When there were clues in the show, such as street signs and signs on buildings, it made my job of locating that place much easier. There were times when there was nothing identifying the location. That made my job much harder. Through the use of google maps, historicaerials.com, newspapers (*Van Nuys News* and *Los Angeles Times*), and telephone directories, I have been able to locate and confirm about 600 locations used in the show.

I hope you enjoy this stroll in time through Southern California. Much of what was is still there. Other locations have changed drastically. Although it was a very time-consuming task to identify, locate, and photograph the locations, it is with pleasure that I present the results of my research to the general public.

# How to Use This Book

This book is setup with an alphabetical listing of locations, mostly by street name, a few by location name (such as Griffith Park and Chavez Ravine). There is no index because it would have been redundant due to the several lists included in this book. The Table of Contents will act as a major index feature. The episode guides and location guide in Appendix A will also act as an index. If you know the location you wish to view, you can find it in the Table of Contents and see the page number it starts on. If you wish to find out what locations were used in a specific episode, look in Appendix A's "Episode Guide—Alphabetical Order with Locations". If you wish to see what episodes were used at a specific location, look in Appendix A's "Location Guide". An additional list is found in Appendix A— "Episode Guide in Broadcast Order". This is simply a listing of the episodes by season in the order originally broadcast.

Each page of the main section of the book is setup in a specific manner, with slight variations. The Then images from the episodes will usually appear in a column on the left side of the page and the Now images are opposite in the right column. Sometimes, the Then image is enlarged and at the top while the Now image is on the bottom, one location image per page. A few of the other pages have been setup differently from the above two varieties. They should be self-explanatory.

# THE STUDIO

# ZIV STUDIO

Located at 7324 Santa Monica Blvd, across the street from United Artists/Goldwyn Studios, this studio was built by King Vidor in 1920. Through a succession of owners, including Grand National and PRC, ZIV Television purchased the studio in 1954. The lot did not have a backlot, so to speak (one row of false fronts were attached to a sound stage), but every inch of exterior space was used on the studio grounds.

The aerial shot above shows the studio lot in early 1954, just prior to its purchase by ZIV. At the time it was owned by Eagle-Lion Pathe.

While all 156 episodes used the sound stages during production, 28 episodes used the studio grounds: "Bank Messenger", "Careless Cop", "Cargo Hi Jack", "Convict's Wife", "Credit Card", "Desperate Men", "Explosives", "Fear", "Fisherman's Luck", "Frightened Witness", "Gem Robbery" (Season 2), "Hitchhiker", "Hitchhiker Dies", "Hot Dust", "Illegal Entry", "The Judge", "Lady Bandits", "Machine-Napping", "Motorcycle" (Season 1), "Plant Robbery", "Prospector", "Runaway Boy", "Scared Cop", "Slain Cabby", "Stolen Car Ring", "Trojan Horse", "The Trucker", and "Typhoid Carrier".

Above is another angle of the studio as seen in stock footage from the "Czar of the Underworld" episode of *Adventures of Superman*. The false front cityscape can be seen along the first floor of the 3-story building in the middle right of the image. The main entrance to the lot and the long ramp alongside sound stages 2 and 3 are just below center. Below is what the property looked like in 2013.

Two-thirds of the lot property was converted into the Movietown Plaza shopping center. That plaza has now been removed and housing will take its place.

The top four images show the false front cityscape set as seen in "Runaway Boy", "Prospector", "The Judge", and "Plant Robbery". The bottom two images show the office buildings on the north side of the lot as seen in "Fisherman's Luck" and "Prospector".

The top row shows the main entrance ("Hot Dust" and "Trojan Horse"). Middle row shows the gas station set (in front of the enclosed incinerator) and the Production and Music building ("Fisherman's Luck" and "Trojan Horse"). The bottom left image location was between the middle row buildings ("Slain Cabby"), while the bottom right image location was also in the same location but with the camera facing the reverse direction ("Frightened Witness").

The Office Buildings

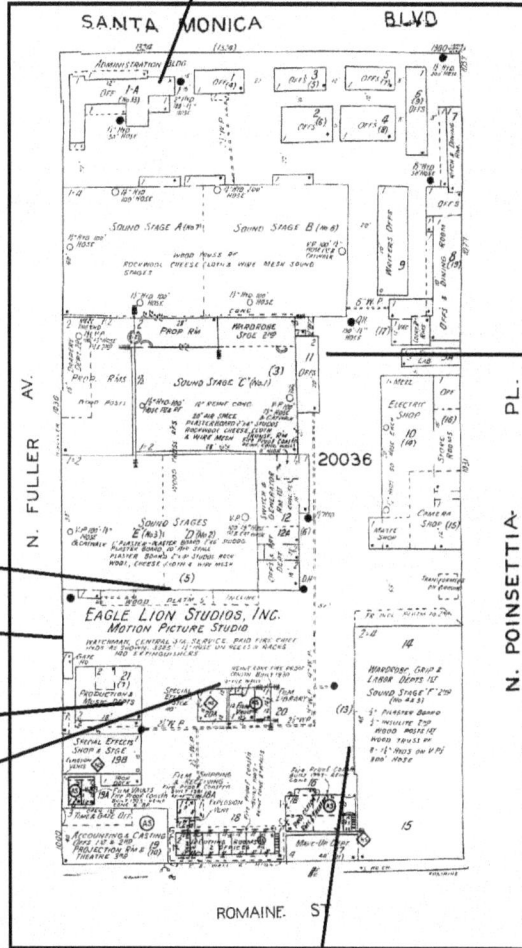

Offices near
Sound Stage
Ramp

The Sound Stage with
the long ramp

The Entrance

The Production and
Music Building

The Gas Station

The False Fronts

This Sanborn Fire Insurance Map was last updated during the Eagle-Lion period. American National purchased the studio from them and they enlarged and/or rebuilt sound stages A and B, expanding the width of them until they reached the Dining building. A ramp was installed to the sound stage next to Office building #11.

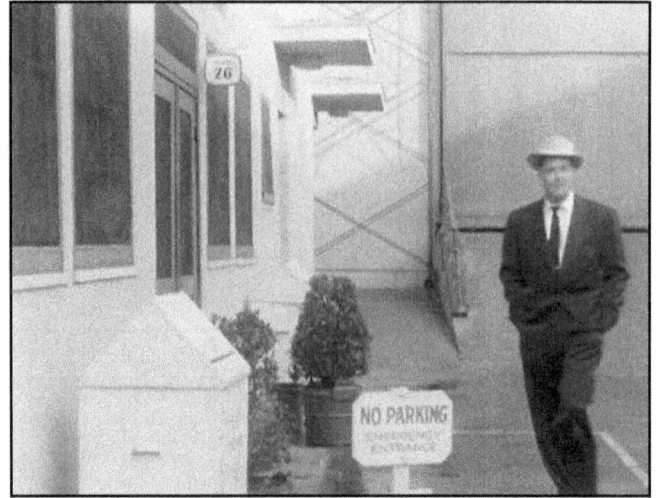

The office building next to Sound Stages A and B after expansion ("Hitchhiker Dies" and "Deperate Men")

A view of the long ramp alongside the sound stage near the entrance (entrance to left) as seen in "Lady Bandits".

# LOS ANGELES COUNTY

## 1st STREET and ARDEN BOULEVARD

This intersection is located a couple of blocks west of Larchmont Boulevard (the area is referred to as Larchmont District) and is located in Los Angeles. The area is little changed since the "Chain Store" episode was filmed.

Arden Boulevard south to 1st Street

Turning right onto 1st Street

Heading west on 1st Street

9

## 2nd STREET and BEACHWOOD DRIVE
This intersection is located one block east and one block south of 1st Street and Arden Boulevard and is located in Los Angeles. The area is little changed since the "Chain Store" episode was filmed.

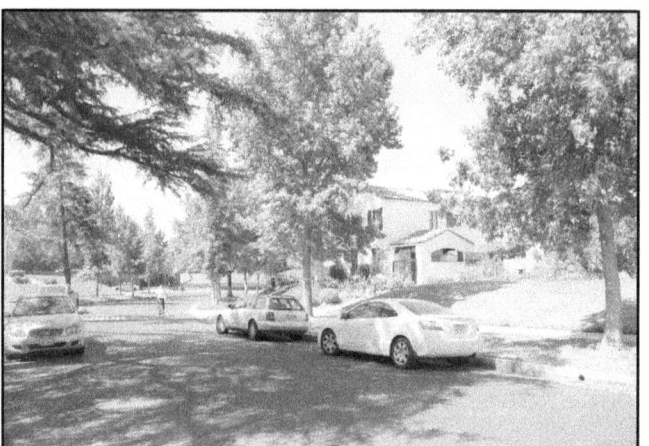

This residential area is located in the city of Carson. It appeared in only one episode: "Auto Press".

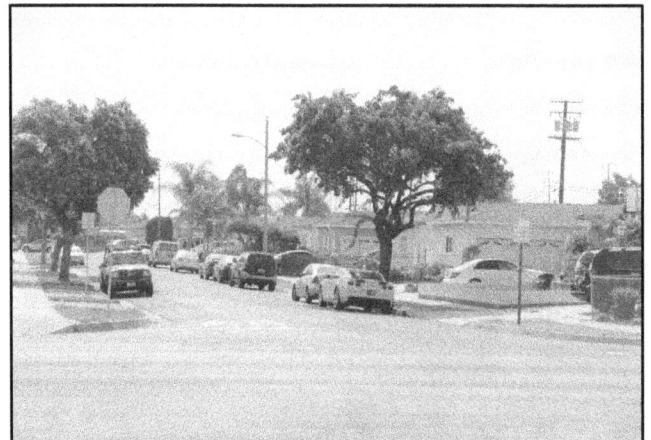

**701 E. 222nd Street**

## 835 ACADEMY ROAD

Located at this address is the Elysian Park Adaptive Recreation Center. It appeared in two episodes: "Hitch Hiker" and "Illegal Entry". It is located across the street from the north end of the Dodger Stadium property (more on Dodger Stadium in the Chavez Ravine section).

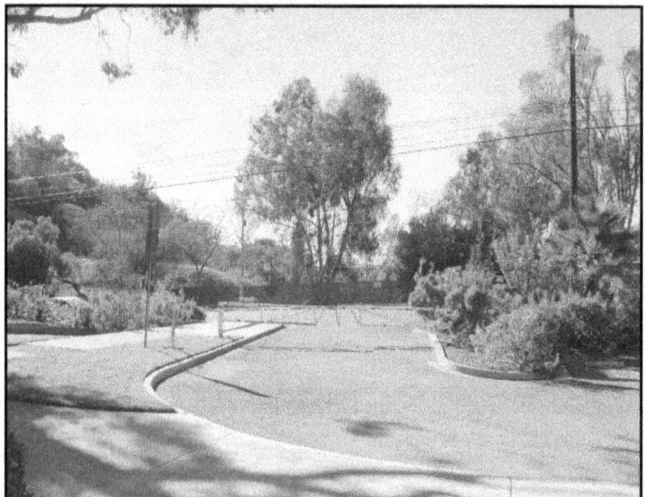

# 1880 ACADEMY ROAD

Located near Dodger Stadium, this is the home of the Los Angeles Police Academy. It appeared in "Hideout".

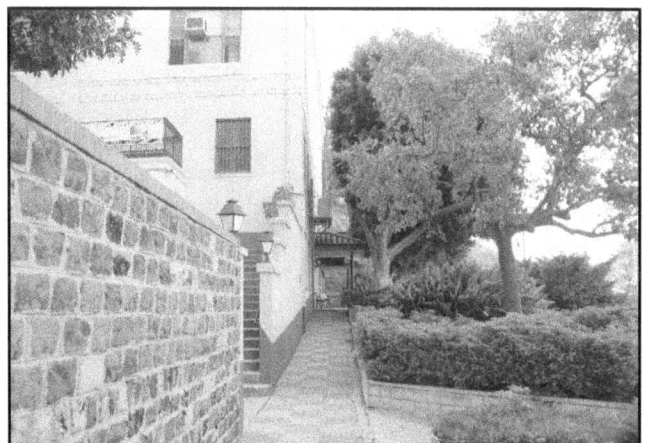

Above are views of the front (south) side of the main building which fronts on Academy Road (originally located at the end of Malvina Avenue)

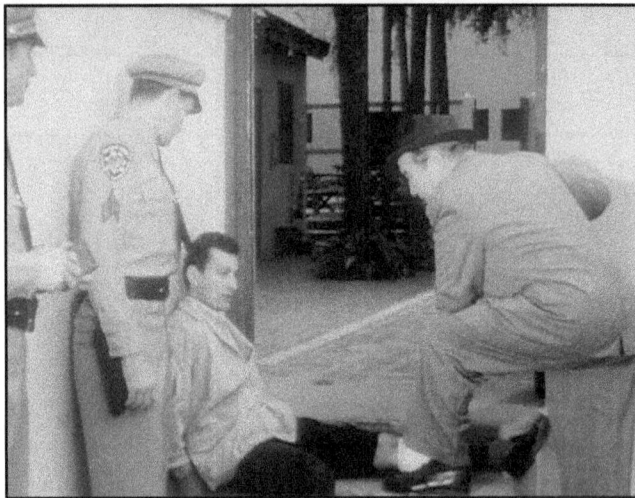

Above is a view of the courtyard on the left (west) side of the main Academy building as seen from the front. Below is a historical view of the area from May 1959.

## 29001 AGOURA ROAD

This location was across the street from Seminole Hot Springs Inn (see next page). There was a restaurant, gas station, and other businesses. It is long gone. It was located on the northwest corner of Agoura Road and Cornell Road in Agoura Hills.

*Top* is a current view of the site. *Above left* shows the restaurant portion of the building. *Above right* shows the entire site along Agoura Road. Across the street (to the left in the above right image) were competing businesses (see 29008 Agoura Road).

This site was used in "Desert Town", "Frightened Witness", "Phony Insurance", and "Prisoner Exchange Copter".

## 29008 AGOURA ROAD

This location was known as Seminole Hot Springs Inn. There was a restaurant, gas station, and other businesses. It was located on the southwest corner of Agoura Road and Cornell Road in Agoura Hills.

*Top* is a current view of the site.
*Above left* shows the left side of the front.
*Above right* shows the side along Cornell Road.
*Right* show the backside of the buildings.
Used in "Frightened Witness", "Human Bomb", "Phony Insurance", "Road-Block", and "Prisoner Exchange Copter".

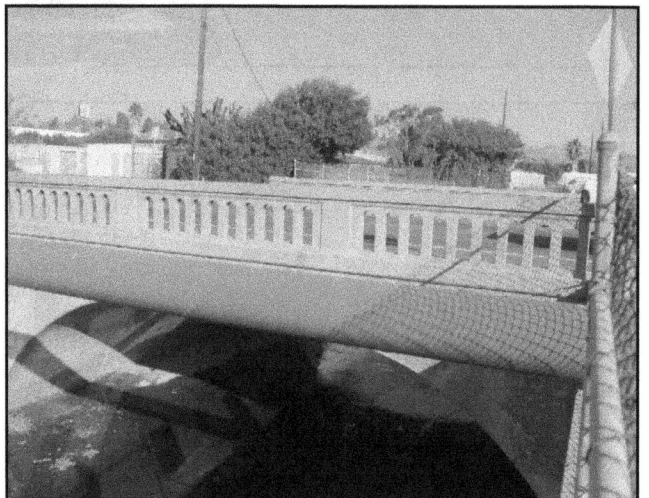

This location was seen in "Frightened Witness" and "Prisoner Exchange Copter".

## ALPINE STREET

An east-west street located south of Elysian Park/Dodger Stadium and north of Sunset Boulevard, all west of the 710 Pasadena Freeway. Two fourth season episodes filmed on the street—a few scenes for "Lady Bandits" and several scenes for "False Confession".

The house was located at 1117 Alpine Street. The alley ran north from Alpine. It was between 1117 on the east and 1119 on the west ("False Confession").

# ALPINE STREET AERIAL

Apartment Building

Alley    1117

Sunset Boulevard

Alpine Street

1041    1037    1033

Joe Tommaso Market was located at 1041 Alpine Street. It was used for both "Lady Bandits" (top left) and "False Confession". While the exterior of the building has changed, this location is confirmed by the house next door with the stone pillar on the corner of the property and in "False Confession", when the bad guys depart the location, they immediately turn the corner. The Pat & Joe's Meat Market just down the street was a possibility for the location when I first was looking for the building which was used in both episodes.

In "False Confessions", Crawford's patrol car parks next to an apartment building (top left). That building was built some time after 1948 and was gone by 1972. For a number of years, the property housed the Los Angeles Department of Water and Power. It is now home to a church. Where the apartment stood is now a parking lot. Also, in "False Confessions", when the Highway Patrol arrives at 1117 Alpine Street and you look eastward along Alpine Street, you can see an oil well to the right of the house (above left). While the house remains, the oil well has been removed. However, the land on which it sat is still vacant.

Alpine Street also appeared in a few episodes where Centennial Street meets it. That intersection is covered in the Centennial Street section.

# ALVARADO STREET

Located about a mile west of Elysian Park, the Harry E. McConnell Service Station was located at 1000 N. Alvarado Street (about a block south of Sunset Boulevard). While the gas station has been gone since about 1962, the building still looks about the same.

# AMESBURY ROAD
Located in the hills below Griffith Park, the exterior of the house at 3660 Amesbury Road and the street leading up to it were used in "Double Death".

**Andora Avenue is located in Chatsworth. It runs diagonally from Topanga Canyon Boulevard to Devonshire Street in a northeast to southwest direction.**

The intersection of Andora Avenue and Faralone Avenue
("Revenge" season 3).

The house above was at the north side of the intersection of Andora Avenue and Faralone Avenue. The house is long gone although a newer house sits on the property ("Revenge" season 3).

The aerial below, looking south, shows just to the right of center and up from center where the diagonal street crosses a vertical street the location of the house. The diagonal street is Andora Avenue and the vertical street on the right is Faralone Avenue. The vertical street on the left is Topanga Canyon Boulevard. At the bottom of the aerial on the left side between two large trees is a whitish house. That house is shown on the next page.

This house, located at 10637 Andora Avenue, was used in "Resident Officer". Above right shows the rear of the house. Above left shows the front, which faces away from Andora Avenue. Left is the garage, which can be seen in the top current photo.

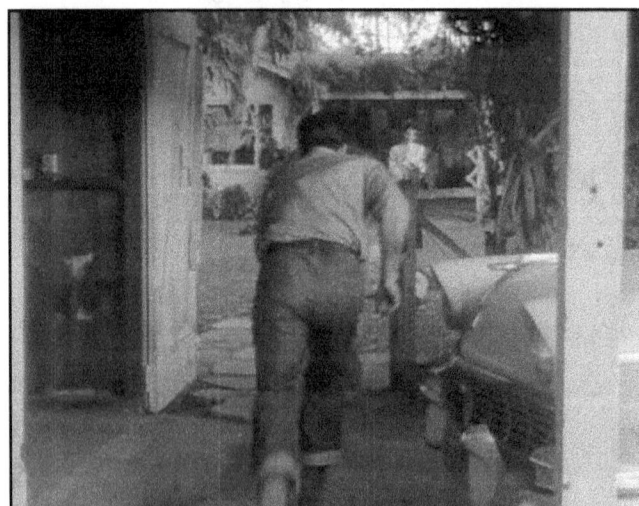

# ANTIOCH STREET

**Antioch Street is located in Pacific Palisades. Only a one block stretch was used in the episode "Harbor Story".**

The bank was located at 15301 Antioch Street. The hardware store was located at 15328 Antioch Street. The alley between buildings was between 15317 Antioch and 910 Via De La Paz.

Located in Woodland Hills, the stretch of road from Highway 101 (now the Ventura Freeway) in the 22800 block to the 22321 block was used in "The Trap". Further eastward on Avenue San Luis, you will meet up with Topanga Canyon Boulevard. Another episode filmed at that intersection and you will find out about it in the Topanga Canyon Boulevard section.

In the top left image, you can just see the exit from Highway 101 (now the Ventura Freeway) onto Avenue San Luis. The house on the corner of Avenue San Luis and Fallbrook Avenue is still there, although hidden by trees, bushes, and a fence.

Above is the view of the intersection of Avenue San Luis and Shoup Avenue as seen in "The Trap". To the left and below are current views of that intersection. The house in the top left image is still there, although hidden by a large structure built in 2011. The house on the hill to the right is also still there.

# BABCOCK AVENUE

Located in the Los Angeles community of Valley Village, 5150 Babcock Avenue is situated on the SE corner of Babcock Avenue and Magnolia Boulevard. While the "Loan Co. office" building is long gone, the houses facing it as well as a building across Magnolia Boulevard from it are still here and look about the same as when "Phony Cop" filmed here.

# BALBOA BOULEVARD

Balboa Boulevard is one of the major north-south arteries of the San Fernando Valley area of Los Angeles County. The three episodes which filmed along it, "Female Hitchhiker", "Hot Rod", and "The 7th Green", were shot in the cities of Granada Hills and Van Nuys. "The 7th Green" was filmed at the Knollwood Country Club on Balboa Boulevard in Granada Hills, but we will look at it in its own section later in the book.

The "Good Food" and "Home Made Pies" belonged to Jeb's Restaurant located at 7600 Balboa Boulevard on the northeast corner of Saticoy Street in Van Nuys. Across the street was Monahan's Inn at 16848 Saticoy Street. Used in "Hot Rod".

These apartments are located at 10727 N. Balboa Boulevard in Granada Hills. Just to the south (to the left) is the building seen on the facing page. Across the street are the houses seen in the background shots on page 34. Used in "Female Hitchhiker".

The Spudnut Donut Shop was located at 10705 N. Balboa Boulevard in Granada Hills. A glimpse of the adjacent apartments can be seen on the right side of both images on this page. Used in "Female Hitchhiker".

Across the street from the apartments were a row of houses. The same houses are there still, with slightly remodeled exteriors. They are located at 10718 to 10732 N. Balboa Boulevard in Granada Hills. Used in "Female Hitchhiker".

The Perrygraf Slide-Chart office was located at 150 S. Barrington Avenue on the second floor. The stairways have been reconfigured into a single tread down to street level and are closed off from the first floor business. Used in "The Christmas Story".

## BEACHWOOD DRIVE

Beachwood Drive in the Hollywood Hills was the gateway to Hollywoodland, a real estate development. *Invasion of the Body Snatchers* (1956) used its streets for some chase scenes near the end of that film. *Highway Patrol* filmed four episodes on that one street: "Art Robbery", "Blast Area-Copter", "Mother's March", and "Rabies".

From top to bottom: 2330, 2400, and 2408 N Beachwood Drive ("Art Robbery").

Continuing the traveling shot on the facing page from "Art Robbery", from top to bottom, we pass 2408 to 2420 N. Beachwood Drive.

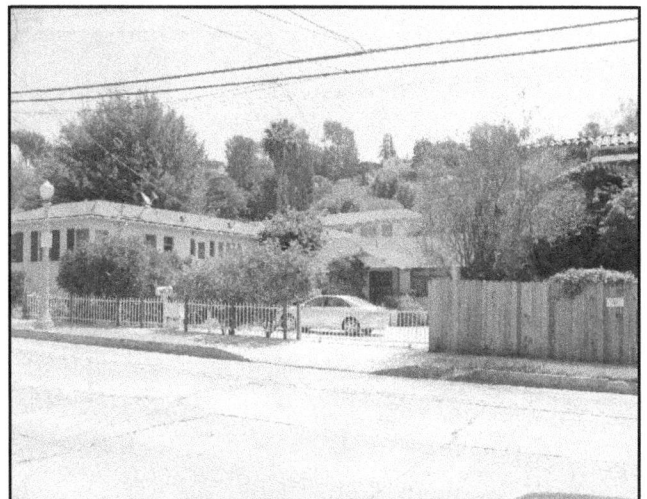

*Below:* The traveling shot stops at the apartments at 2438 N. Beachwood Drive.

*Above:* The alley used in "Mother's March" is located between 2673 and 2677 N. Beach-wood Drive

*Below:* The alley above curves around to the north to this alley which is located on the south side of 2691 N. Beachwood Drive ("Mother's March")

*Above:* The main entrance into the old Hollywoodland tract features arches on both sides of the street. Here we see it in "Mother's March". *Below:* Heading south from the arches, the patrol car heads towards Glen Oak ("Mother's March").

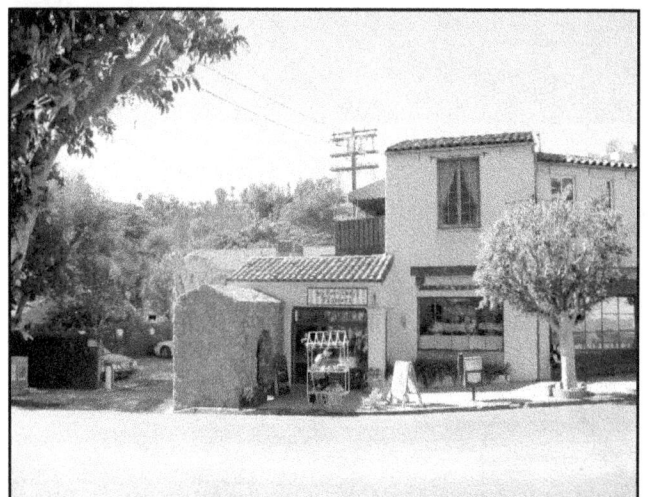

The Hill-Top Beauty Salon was a real establishment at the time of filming on "Mother's March". It was located at 2691 N. Beachwood Drive.

Across the street from 2691 N. Beachwood Drive was a Richfield Gas Station (at 2694) which was used in "Blast Area-Copter". Richfield became Atlantic-Richfield, then Arco. The gas station is no longer there.

In "Mother's March", ladies go door-to-door raising funds. Below is there stop at 2800 N. Beachwood Drive.

The house above was located at 2837 N. Beachwood Drive and was across the street from the house below which was located at 2838 N. Beachwood Drive. While the above house looks about the same, the below house has been heavily renovated and the front facade looks entirely different. Used in "Mother's March".

In "Rabies", the patrol car arrived at the above house by traveling down the street (below). After finding no one home, they exited the area by driving up the street. The house is located at 3074 N. Beachwood Drive. This area is near the end of the public paved street. A horse ranch and hiking trails can be found further up the canyon.

# BEAUDRY AVENUE

This street begins at Figueroa Terrace, just below Elysian Park and Dodger Stadium and runs south. The section at the north end was used in "False Confessions".

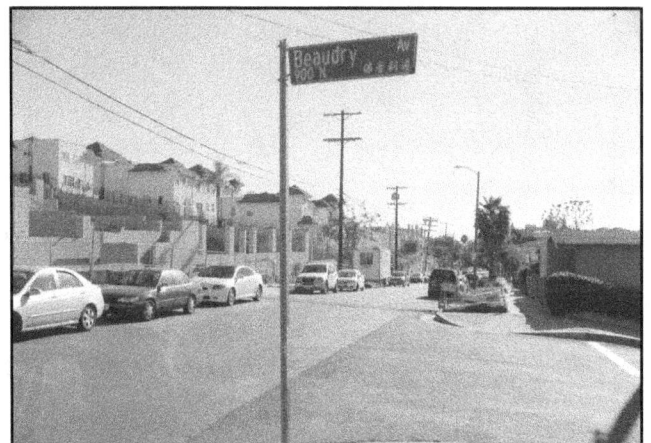

## BELDEN DRIVE

Belden Drive is located in Hollywoodland. It connects at an intersection with Beachwood Drive and Westshire Drive. The Texaco gas station was located at 2707 Belden Drive. It is long gone. The buildings along Westshire Drive at Beachwood Drive are still there.

The location of the Texaco gas station can be seen in the still on the facing page from *Invasion of the Body Snatchers*. The Richfield gas station at 2694 N. Beachwood Drive is to the left front (out of the picture). The two buildings on the facing page are on the right side, a small portion barely viewable.

Broderick Crawford talking on the radio on the facing page is a scene from "Mother's March". The Texaco station is from "Rabies".

## BENEDICT CANYON DRIVE

One of many canyon communities in the hills of Los Angeles County, it has changed greatly since the 1950's as wealthy homeowners have moved in and, for many of the original homes, replaced them with more costly homes. The property at 2727 Benedict Canyon Drive is one such place, used in two episodes ("Taxi" and "Kidnap-Copter"). Originally a small brick home and a small cabin is now two large mansions. Among the owners of the location in recent years are Cher and Eddie Murphy.

The property is on the side of a hill. The house was on the upper portion of the property. The cabin was a little ways down slope from the house. Both were accessed by the same entry road. The entire property has now changed and it is gated and completely private. Images are from "Taxi".

In the right image, you can see the house in the background as Matthews approaches the cabin.

Top image is from "Kidnap-Copter" and the bottom one from "Taxi".

*Above:* House is located at 1495 Benedict Canyon Drive ("Taxi").

*Above:* The street heading off up the hill on the right is Clear View Drive ("Taxi").
*Below:* A better angle of the houses near Clear View Drive ("Taxi").

Located in the city of Beverly Hills, Beverly Drive connects with Franklin Canyon Drive (see Franklin Canyon section). Two houses on the street had exteriors filmed at them: 1344 and 1364. The latter house has been removed and a newer, larger house has replaced it. These houses were used in the "Revenge" episode from Season 4.

Above is the drive up Beverly Drive pass 1344, which is still there, and the arrival at 1364 which has been replaced.

The house at 1450 N. Beverly Drive still looks the same from when it was used by Robert Conrad for his mother's house in "Revenge" (Season 4).

## BEVERLY GLEN BOULEVARD

This route through the Hollywood Hills begins at Ventura Boulevard in the San Fernando Valley and heads south to its terminus at Pico Boulevard in Los Angeles. The restaurant (see below—"Careless Cop") at 2181 N. Beverly Glen Boulevard is in the hills, while the apartments (see next page) in and around 1643 S. Beverly Glen Boulevard are near Santa Monica Boulevard.

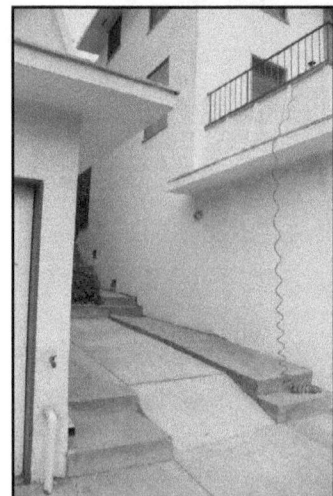

The apartments in and around 1643 S. Beverly Glen Boulevard have changed very little since "Portrait of Death" was filmed there.

## BRAND BOULEVARD

The city of San Fernando was used in two episodes, and Brand Boulevard appeared in both. The then San Fernando High School (now Junior High) at 130 N. Brand Boulevard was seen in "Escort" and the Hotel Goodhap at 208 S. Brand Boulevard is seen in "Machine-Napping".

The telephone booth above was located in what is now the middle of the parking lot at 1708 N. Bronson Avenue. The buildings across the street are still there. All then images on this page are from "Missing Witness".

The Bronsonia Apartments, now known as the Bronson Towers, 1933 N. Bronson Avenue
("The Collector")

**An east-west street in the San Fernando Valley. Filming took place along it in the cities of Valley Village and Sherman Oaks in "The Search" and "Slain Cabby".**

The Hickory House was located at 12105 Burbank Boulevard on the northwest corner wit Laurel Canyon Boulevard. Across the street at 12116 Burbank Boulevard was the Sego Nursery. The nursery is still there, but the Hickory House building has been demoilished and another eatery is on the corner. Used in "The Search".

In "Slain Cabby", a one-block section of Burbank Boulevard in Sherman Oaks was used. Above is the north side of the street in the 1300 block.

In "Slain Cabby", a one-block section of Burbank Boulevard in Sherman Oaks was used. Above is the south side of the street in the 1300 block. Nory's Gifts & Jewelry was at 13644, now the right end of the Robin Hood British Pub Restaurant, while the Wardwell Hardware was at 13636, now the entrance to IIS Insurance Services.

# CALABASAS ROAD

Calabasas Road in Calabasas now runs the entire length of the city. However, when *Highway Patrol* filmed there, the street was not continuous. Where Mureau Road now crosses the 101 Freeway and connects with Calabasas Road, that is just a few feet from where Calabasas Road stopped before beginning again a few hundred yards to the east. It is the eastern section where "Gambling" used the exit from Highway 101 and the highway frontage area as seen below.

This intersection is located in the hills of Woodland Hills. The "Released Convict" episode shot all around these hills.

## CAMPO ROAD and PROVIDENCIA STREET
This intersection is located in the hills of Woodland Hills. The "Released Convict" episode shot all around these hills. The cement pad for the original garage can be seen in the now photo below.

# CANYON DRIVE

Canyon Drive runs from the Hollywood Freeway (with a short stretch below the freeway) up into the Hollywood Hills of Griffith Park. The Bronson Canyon Caves are near the end of the paved road (an unpaved hiking trail continues into the hills above). This street and the caves were used in a number of episodes: "Art Robbery", "Blast Area-Copter", "The Collector", "Copter Cave In", "Insulin", "Missing Witness", "Officer's Wife", "Prisoner Exchange Copter", "Prospector", "Stolen Plane-Copter", and "Wounded".

*Above:* An alley runs from Bronson Avenue on the west to Canyon Drive on the east between Carlton Way on the north and Harold Way on the south, as seen in "The Collector".

*Above:* In "Insulin", there is a traveling shot on Canyon Drive at Bronson Hill Drive.

2239 Canyon Drive in "Wounded"

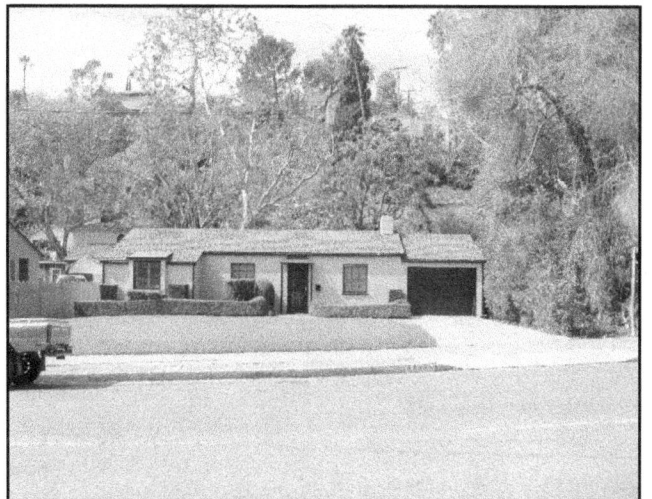

2245 Canyon Drive in "Insulin"

2606 Canyon Drive is barely visible in "Wounded" on the left

2633 Canyon Drive in "The Collector"

2707 Canyon Drive in "Missing Witness"

The entrance into Bronson Canyon

## BRONSON CANYON

Bronson Canyon and the Caves are located north of the residential area of Canyon Drive. The road is paved up to the entrance to the Hollywoodland Girl's Camp. Beyond that is an unpaved hiking trail into the hills. Nine episodes used the canyon and caves: "Art Robbery", "Blast Area-Copter", "Copter Cave In", "Human Bomb", "Insulin", "Missing Witness", "Prisoner Exchange Copter", "Prospector", and "Stolen Plane-Copter".

A short distance up Canyon Drive from the entrance to the park (see facing page bottom images) is a fair sized parking area. *Highway Patrol* used the parking area for helicopter landings and takeoffs, and for one episode, "Human Bomb", as a place to detonate a bomb.

*Top:* "Prospector"
*Bottom:* "Art Robbery"

*Top:* Canyon Drive with the side road to the caves ("Blast Area-Copter")
*Middle:* Where the cave side road and Canyon Drive meet ("Art Robbery")
*Bottom:* The side road to the caves ("Prisoner Exchange Copter")

*Top:* "Prisoner Exchange Copter"
*Middle:* "Stolen Plane-Copter"
*Bottom:* "Stolen Plane-Copter"

*Top:* The road to the caves
*Middle:* To the left side of the front cave
*Bottom:* The front cave

The front cave goes to the back along a tunnel where two branches fork off to left and right to create 3 exits on the other side of the hill.

*Top:* Rounding the cliff from the front to the back. Uncareful camera angles will show the Hollywood sign ("Blast Area-Copter")
*Middle:* Heading into the back cave area ("Insulin")
*Bottom:* A view from the inside out the front cave entrance ("Stolen Plane-Copter")

The right cave entrance was large enough
for a car to drive through

The 3 cave entrances

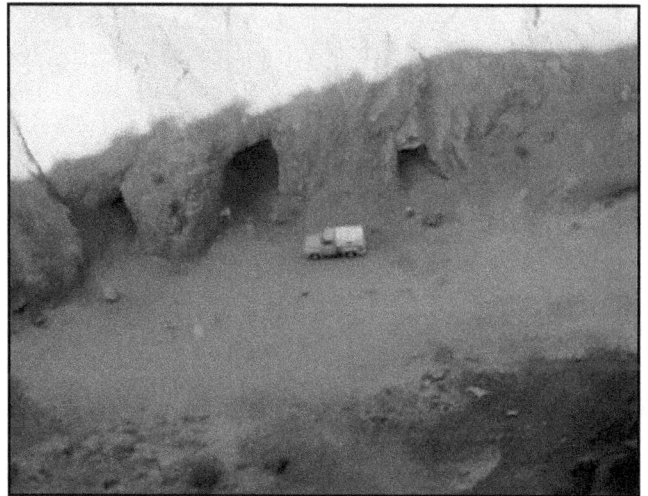

*Top:* "Copter Cave In"
*Middle:* "Prisoner Exchange Copter"
*Bottom:* "Copter Cave In"

## CELIS STREET

Located in the city of San Fernando, Celis Street between San Fernando Mission Boulevard and Kalisher Street is now a shopping center. Only the J.C. Penney store on Celis Street remains of the buildings which appeared in "Machine-Napping".

Walking eastward on Celis Street towards Brand Boulevard ("Machine-Napping")

Rounding the corner of Celis Street onto Brand Boulevard ("Machine-Napping")

# CENTENNIAL STREET

Centennial Street runs three blocks, from Figueroa Terrace on the north and Alpine Street on the south. It appears in "Bank Messenger", "Confidence Game", and "Lady Bandits".

The Mayo Motel was located at 840 N. Figueroa Street, a block east of the above intersection. The motel encompassed an entire city block. "Bank Messenger" used the motel for several scenes—above is the southwest corner of the motel property.

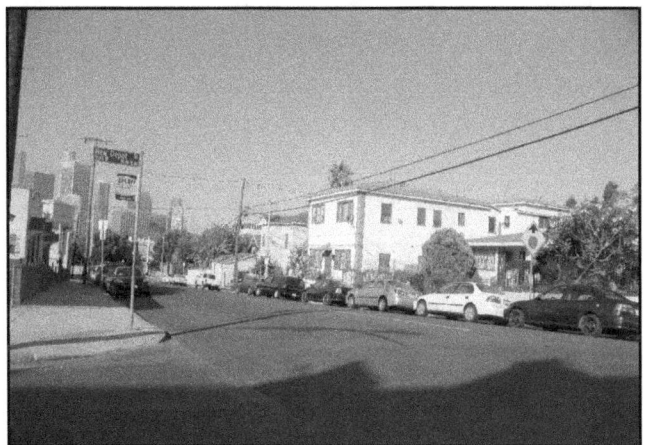

Heading up Centennial Street from Alpine Street to New Depot Street as seen in "Bank Messenger".

*Top:* Centennial Street and Alpine Street ("Confidence Game")
*Middle:* Centennial Street and Alpine Street ("Lady Bandits")
*Bottom:* Outside 802 Centennial Street ("Lady Bandits")

# CENTRAL AVENUE

**Located in Glendale, this street is one of the major routes north-south through the city. Filming took place near San Fernando Road and Railroad Street.**

"Hostage" used Central Avenue (see above) from the intersection with Railroad Street and eastward to Gardena Avenue.

The Central Motel was located at 1516 S. Central Avenue, at the intersection with San Fernando Road. While the motel has been replaced by a high-rise medical building, the furniture store across the street is still there. "Express Delivery" used this location.

**SOUTHERN PACIFIC GLENDALE DEPOT and CERRITOS AVENUE**
Located in Glendale, the west end of the street dead ends at the old Southern Pacific
Train Depot. The road approaching the depot from the east is Cerritos Avenue.

The top two images are from "Express Delivery". They show Cerritos Avenue just to the east of the depot. The bottom image is from "Hostage" and shows the old exit while the now photo shows the current exit. Gardena Avenue is the cross street. All of the houses on the west side of the street have been removed for the expansion of the depot and area.

*Top:* The front of the station ("Gem Robbery" season 4)
*Middle:* The front of the station ("Suicide")
*Bottom:* A baggage/storge room entrance on the front side ("Express Delivery")

*Top:* The ornate front door to the depot ("Suicide")
*Middle:* The rear of the station facing the tracks ("Hostage")
*Bottom:* The north parking area ("Hostage")

# CHATSWORTH STREET

A semi-major east-west road north of Devonshire Boulevard, a portion of it west of Topanga Canyon Boulevard was used in "Female Hitchhiker" and "Resident Officer". This street was just north of the house at 10637 Andora Avenue which was also used in "Resident Officer". All filming was in the city of Chatsworth.

*Top to Bottom:* Chatsworth Street from Topanga Canyon Boulevard on the east to Farralone Street on the west

*Both:* Chatsworth Street looking north

At the time of filming, Topanga Canyon Boulevard ended at Devonshire Street which was several streets to the south of Chatsworth Street. The end of Topanga Canyon Boulevard was the beginning of Santa Susana Pass Road.

# CHAVEZ RAVINE

Nestled in the hills just north of downtown Los Angeles and surrounded by Elysian Park and the city of Los Angeles, "Chavez Ravine" was home to thousands. Now it is home to Dodger Stadium. What we refer to as "Chavez Ravine" was actually Sulphur Ravine and Cemetery Ravine. Chavez Ravine still exists on the west side of Dodger Stadium. The "Chavez Ravine" area has changed drastically from the late 1950's when it was used in twelve episodes during Seasons 3 and 4: "Bank Messenger", "Confidence Game", "Credit Card", "Dan Hostage", "Dead Hunter", "Deaf Mute", "Family Affair", "Fear", "Hideout", "Hostage Officer", "Illegal Entry", and "Lady Bandits". This change, which will be shown graphically on the following pages, was the result of the Federal Housing Act of 1949, which gave to cities money to build low-income housing. Los Angeles decided to create Elysian Park Heights where "Chavez Ravine" was located. Using eminent domain, the city began foreclosing and buying the property of the inhabitants of the three, mainly Mexican-American, communities of Palo Verde, La Loma, and Bishop, in order to clear the land and erect 24 13-story buildings and more than 160 2-story townhouses as well as rebuilding the schools and playgrounds in the area. By 1953, most of the area had been cleared of housing. Then a new mayor was elected—and he stopped the redevelopment. In the late 1950's, the Dodger baseball team came to Los Angeles, and the city sold to them the "Chavez Ravine" land. By the end of 1959, all residents of "Chavez Ravine" (actually, Sulphur Ravine and Cemetery Ravine) were gone and the Dodgers began construction on their facility. This included bulldozing the top off of Lookout Mountain (the lower part of it is behind the home plate area of the stadium) and other areas. Sulphur Ravine and Cemetery Ravine were filled in—the two-story Palo Verde Elementary School was filled with dirt then covered. It sits under a parking lot at the stadium as well as the entire "Chavez Ravine" residential areas—all under Dodger Stadium. Except for a couple of photos of the parking lot, there is no possible way to show the now portion of this area. So, using images from the show, historic maps of the area, including aerial shots, and a current aerial, I will attempt to show approximately where the filming took place.

A street map from the 1950's showing all of the street names and locations in the "Chavez Ravine" area, most of which is now buried beneath Dodger Stadium.

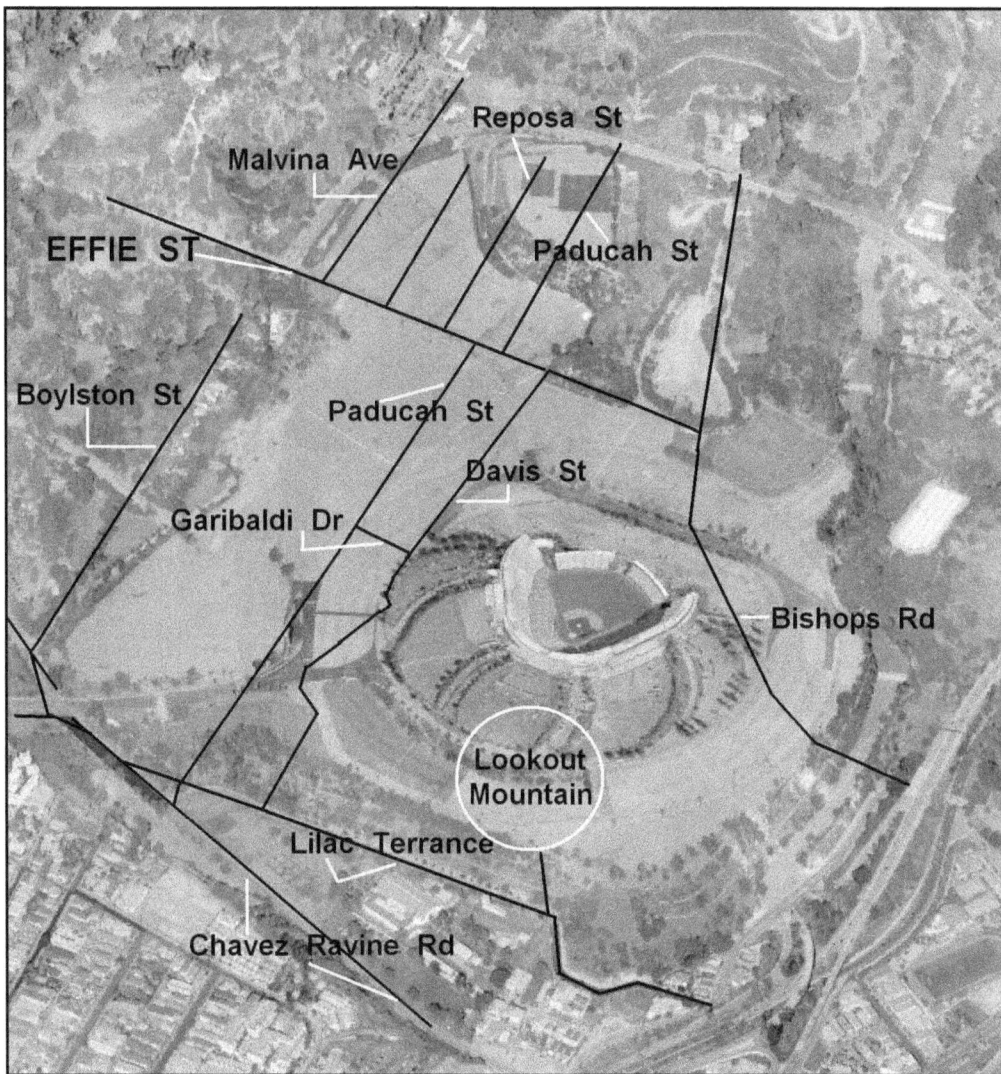

This hill and valley area of Los Angeles, which includes Elysian Park, was comprised of four ravines: Chavez, Sulphur, Cemetery, and Solano. The Solano Ravine area mostly still exists (the southern portion in the hills was removed in 1959). Chavez Ravine is to the west of Dodger Stadium and still exists. Sulphur Ravine included the length of Paducah Street. Cemetery Ravine ran the length of Bishops Road. Hills separated the ravines from one another. Sulphur and Cemetery Ravines were filled in. Sulphur Ravine sits under the western parking lots of Dodger Stadium. Cemetery Ravine sits under the areas to the north and east of the stadium.

The following two pages contains labeled aerial photographs of two sections of this area. The major streets are identified so you can find the approximate locations on those maps with the one above and with the scenes from the show.

Effie Street—Malvina Street—Reposa Street—Paducah Street—Bishops Road

Boylston Street—Paducah Street—Davis Street—Bishops Road

Boylston Street—Garibaldi Street—Paducah Street—Davis Street

Chavez Ravine Road—Paducah Street—Davis Street—Lilac Terrace—Joplin Street

**85**

## BISHOPS ROAD

Now under tons of dirt, Bishops Road ran from the Elysian Park Playground, now the Elysian Park Adaptive Recreation Center at 835 Academy Road, straight down to Effie Street where it curved to the left (southeast) along Lookout Mountain, before ending up at North Broadway. The only portions of this road still in existance, to some extent, are near the 110 freeway underpass to Broadway, and what is now a driveway into the north end of Dodger Stadium opposite the Elysian Park Adaptive Recreation Center.

*Top:* Driving south on Bishops Road toward the 110 freeway just south of the intersection with Effie Street. ("Hostage Officer")

*Middle:* Heading north on Bishops Road near Effie Street. ("Bank Messenger")

*Bottom:* Farther north on Bishops Road. The end of the street is in the distance. ("Bank Messenger")

## BISHOPS ROAD

*Top:* Driving south on Bishops Road, about halfway between the north end and Effie Street. ("Bank Messenger")

*Middle:* Heading south on Bishops Road. The building in the top imagecan be seen on the left. In the background is the north end of the street. ("Hitch Hiker")

*Bottom:* Farther south on Bishops Road, nearing Effie Street. ("Bank Messenger")

## EFFIE STREET

While Effie Street still exists in Los Angeles, for our purposes, it ran from Malvina Street on the west to Bishops Road on the east. Most of this stretch of street was in Sulphur Ravine while a small portion was in Cemetery Ravine.

*Top:* Driving east on Effie Street, nearing Bishops Road. Barely visible in the shot is a side road on the left which can be seen on the next page. ("Deaf Mute")

*Middle:* Turning from Effie Street onto Bishops Road, heading south. ("Hitch Hiker")

*Bottom:* Just turned from Bishops Road onto Effie Street and heading up the hill. ("Hitch Hiker")

**EFFIE STREET**

*Top:* The side road off of Effie Street. The hills in the background still exist at that height, but the floor of the ravine has been greatly raised. ("Family Affair")

*Middle:* This is Bishops Road, heading south. The large white structure on the left is at the corner of Effie Street. ("Dan Hostage")

*Bottom:* After coming over the hill (see facing page top) on Effie Street, you will pass the Palo Verde Elementary School (seen behind the patrol car). This building was not razed—it was filled with dirt, then covered over with the rest of the ravine. It is now under a parking lot of Dodger Stadium. ("Hideout")

*Top:* This grocery store was located at 1146 Effie Street at the intersection with Reposa Street. It was owned by the De Leon family. They also owned the house diagonally across the street. ("Confidence Game")

*Middle:* A historical look at the store when it was still in operation.

*Bottom:* The De Leon family home was on the corner of Effie Street and Reposa Street at 1151 Effie Street. ("Dan Hostage")

## EFFIE STREET

Here are three today images of Effie Street—well, sort of. The street is now quite a ways underground.

*Top:* Effie Street runs about along the fence line. The elementary school was where the bushes are in the middle distance.

*Middle:* The General Store would be located approximately in the middle of the image..

*Bottom:* Malvina Street would be on the left side of this shot.

## BOYLSTON STREET

This street was realigned during construction of Dodger Stadium. Only the south portion and a long stretch of the north end are the same. The area inbetween (the steep grade at left) is no longer a street. The northeast area of the intersection of Boylston Street and Chavez Ravine Road (now Stadium Way) had housing, now long gone.

*Top:* A look at the southern end of Boylston Street as it approaches Chavez Ravine Road. ("Lady Bandits")

*Middle:* A today view of the same area.

*Bottom:* Chavez Ravine Road as it heads east from Boylston Street, barely seen at the left. ("Hostage Officer")

## BOYLSTON STREET

*Top:* Turning into the property from Boylston Street just north of Chavez Ravine Road. ("Lady Bandits")

*Middle:* A view of the back/side of the house. ("Lady Bandits")

*Bottom:* The following year, the house had already been razed. ("Family Affair")

*Top:* A look at the front of the house. ("Lady Bandits")

*Middle:* A closer look at the front of the house. ("Lady Bandits")

*Bottom:* The patrol car is facing the front of the house. The street behind is Chavez Ravine Road. ("Lady Bandits")

## REPOSA STREET
## PADUCAH STREET

*Top:* A look up Reposa Street from Effie Street. The De Leon family home is on the left. ("Dan Hostage")

*Middle:* Located at 1442 Paducah Street, south of Garibaldi Street. ("Confidence Game")

*Bottom:* An historical look at 1442 Paducah Street in 1957. The two youngest kids are two years older in the middle image.

## DAVIS STREET

This street begins at Lilac Terrace on the south and heads north, past Effie Street, to Avalon Street. Below Effie Street, only two streets cross it:: Garibaldi Drive and Joplin Street.

*Top:* The house on the southeast corner of Davis Street and Garibaldi Drive, at 1456. ("Dead Hunter")

*Middle:* A historical look at the house during a 1957 fire.

*Bottom:* The house next door (south side) at 1448. ("Hostage Officer")

# DAVIS STREET

*Top:* Davis Street just north of Garibaldi Drive. ("Lady Bandits")

*Middle:* The intersection of Davis Street and Garibaldi Drive. The street heading away from the patrol car is Garibaldi Drive. ("Credit Card")

*Bottom:* Heading south on Davis Street from Garibaldi Drive. The house at 1456 is to the right. ("Fear")

*Top:* Davis Street at the south end intersection with Lilac Terrace. ("Credit Card")

*Middle:* Davis Street near the intersection with Joplin Street. ("Credit Card")

*Bottom:* Joplin Street heading east from Davis Street. ("Credit Card")

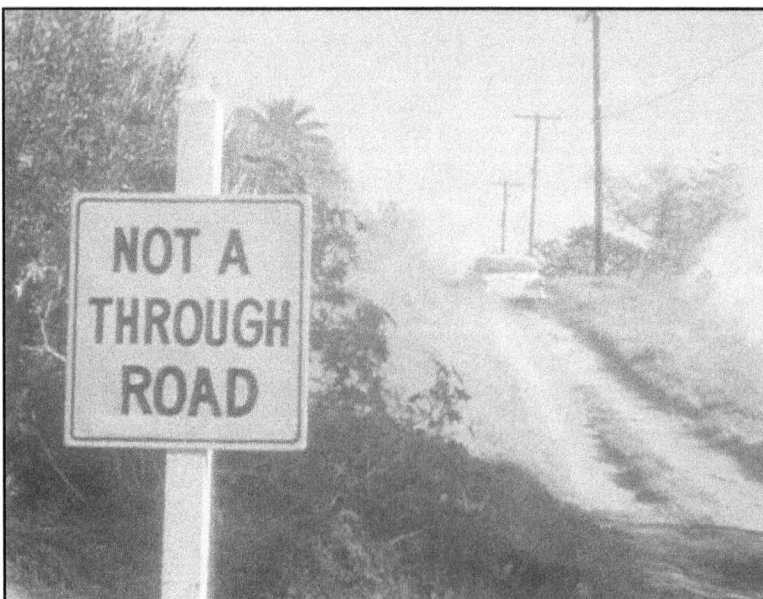

## LILAC TERRACE
## BISHOPS ROAD

Lilac Terrace is at the south side of the Dodger Stadium property. Bishops Road, now Stadium Way, at the 110 Freeway has a different look.

*Top:* Lilac Terrace opposite the old Armory building. You can just see a garage on the left. The house above it was one of the last three purchased by the Dodgers and removed. ("Hitch Hiker")

*Middle:* Bishops Road before you reach Effie Street. You can see the 110 freeway in the upper left portion of the image. ("Hitch Hiker")

*Bottom:* The Bishops Road underpass of the 110 freeway. Where the patrol car is heading west, that street no longer exists (it's under a hill for Dodger Stadium). The road now curves to the right and parallels the freeway. ("Bank Messenger")

99

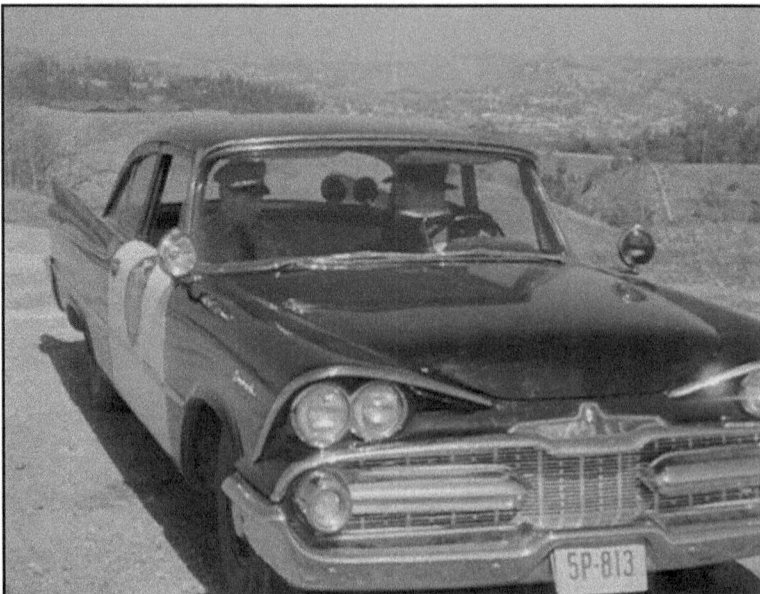

## LOOKOUT MOUNTAIN

Once 726 feet in height, the top was removed during the grading for Dodger Stadium. Part of the hill still remains behind home plate of the stadium as the stadium was built into the side of the hill.

*Top:* Heading up the east side of Lookout Mountain. The intersection of Bishops Road and Effie Street can be seen in the distance. ("Hitch Hiker")

*Middle:* From atop Lookout Mountain, looking northwest toward the L. A. Police Academy. ("Bank Messenger")

*Bottom:* From atop Lookout Mountain, looking northeast. The Solano Reservoir roof can be seen just above the left rear of the patrol car. ("Bank Messenger")

**LOOKOUT MOUNTAIN**

*Top:* Atop Lookout Mountain, looking eastward. You can see Main Street in the background. ("Bank Messenger")

*Middle:* From atop Lookout Mountain, looking southeast. The four tanks were a mainstay of the downtown landscape for many years. All now gone. ("Bank Messenger")

*Bottom:* From atop Lookout Mountain, looking south. The 4-level interchange (101 and 110 freeways) is visible in the background. ("Bank Messenger")

Douglas Park is located in the city of Santa Monica. It's official address is 2439 Wilshire Boulevard. On its west side is Chelsea Avenue. In "Stolen Car Ring", the bad guys park on Chelsea Avenue next to the park, then enter the park.

*Top:* 1124 Chelsea Avenue
*Middle:* 1130 Chelsea Avenue
*Bottom:* Douglas Park

## CHEROKEE AVENUE
This street is located in the Hollywood section of Los Angeles. The Chancellor Apartments are at 1842 North Cherokee Avenue and can be seen in "Released Convict". The De Longpre Park address is 1350 N. Cherokee Avenue. However, "Killer on the Run" used the June Street side (east).

*Top:* 1842 N. Cherokee Avenue
*Middle and Bottom:* De Longpre Park, 1350 N. Cherokee Avenue

*Top:* Across from De Longpre Park, 1340 N. June St
*Bottom:* De Longpre Park

On the previous page, the church steeple in the bottom images belongs to the Blessed Sacrament Church at 6657 Sunset Boulevard where Cherokee Street meets it.

# CHESEBORO ROAD

Located in the outskirts of Palmdale, this road begins just north of Pearblossom Highway and heads south into the mountains to Little Rock Reservoir. Filming on "Desert-Copter" took place on this road and areas off of it. At that time, the road was newly paved and most of the area roads were unpaved.

Pearblossom Highway and Cheseboro Road

Cheseboro Road south of Mt. Emma Road

Cheseboro Road and Mt. Emma Road. The dirt road curving up the hill can barely be seen in the ground level view.

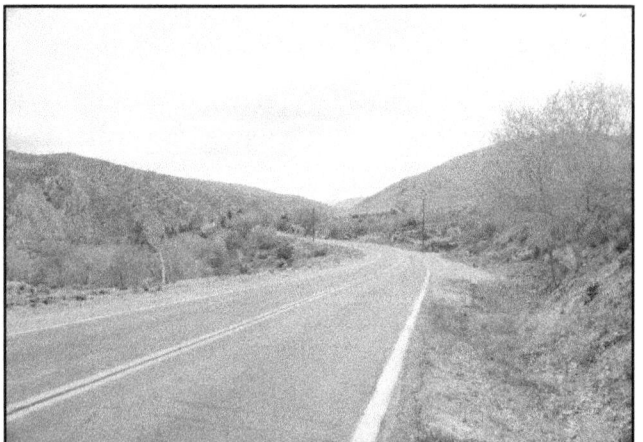

Cheseboro Road from Mt. Emma Road south to the entrance to Little Rock Reservoir Recreation Area.

# CITRUS AVENUE

"Girl Bandit" used the north side of the building located at 915. The exterior of the building has changed somewhat, but based on aerials, the interior has greatly changed, which doesn't matter as the show only used the exterior.

The above now photos show the north side and the east side of the building.

Located in the city of Malibu, this street begins at Malibu Canyon Road and heads south, paralleling Pacific Coast Highway for a bit before heading off farther south.

Scenes from "Harbor Story" along Civic Center Way

# CLARK AVENUE

Located in Burbank, 3711 W. Clark Avenue was used for the real estate office in "License Plates", which was a real Real Estate business. It is now a pre-school.

This is a major north-south artery from the San Fernando Valley to Los Angeles through the Santa Monica Mountains. Two episodes used this street: "Deadly Diamonds" and "Phony Cop".

*Top:* The Colfax Cleaners, 4360 Coldwater Canyon Avenue ("Deadly Diamonds")
*Middle:* 5439 Coldwater Canyon Avenue ("Phony Cop")
*Bottom:* Across from 5439, three airport light towers in background ("Phony Cop")

110

# COLFAX AVENUE
## Located in the San Fernando Valley. "Taxi" was the only episode to use this street.

*Top:* The NW corner of Colfax Avenue and Oxnard Street
*Middle:* 6009 Colfax Avenue
*Bottom:* 6013 Colfax Avenue

*Top:* The NE corner of Colfax Avenue and Oxnard Street
*Middle:* The gas station on the SW corner of the intersection. The building across the street has been replaced by an office building. The now shot is taken from in front of that building.
*Bottom:* Exiting the gas station onto Oxnard Street. The buildings on the NE corner are still there.

## COMMONWEALTH AVENUE

Located in the Los Feliz area of East Hollywood, it paralleled Hillhurst Avenue. A traveling shot for "Double Death" was filmed along the 2100 block.

*Top:* Looking north towards Griffith Park
*Middle:* 2121 N. Commonwealth Avenue
*Bottom:* 2115 N. Commonwealth Avenue

*Above:* 2105 N. Commonwealth Avenue

## COMSTOCK AVENUE

Located in Los Angeles one block east of Beverly Glen Boulevard, the short stretch used in "Portrait of Death" is just north of Santa Monica Boulevard.

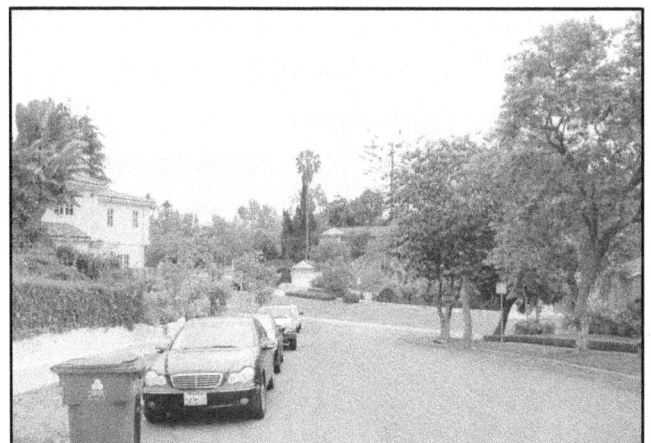

*Top:* Heading north on Comstock Avenue from Santa Monica Boulevard
*Middle:* Just past Eastbourne Avenue heading north
*Bottom:* Heading west on Eastbourne Avenue from Comstock Avenue

**Located in Los Angeles, a short stretch of this street south of Hollywood Boulevard was used in "Brave Boy".**

Very little has changed on this street. The apartments are the same on both sides of the street and the building on the north side of Hollywood Boulevard is the same.

The building in the background of "Radioactive" was located at 200 Culver Boulevard.

The General Store above was located at 185 Culver Boulevard.
It is now "The Shack".

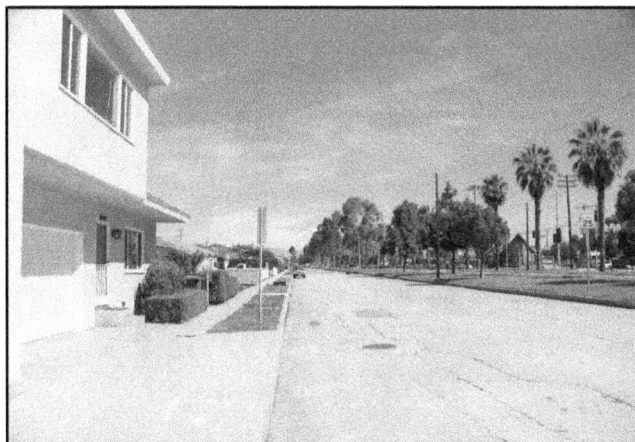

The apartments at 12755 Culver Boulevard and the street eastward from that location were used in "Hit and Run".

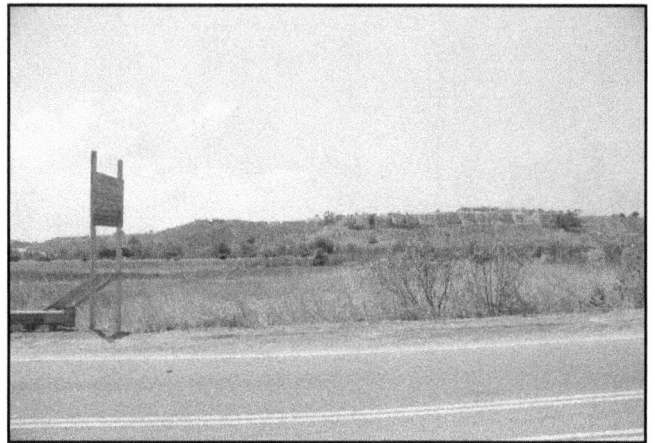

The Culver Boulevard bridge over Ballona Creek is seen in the top images. Near the bridge, the fields and hills to the southside of Culver Boulevard can be seen. If the camera for "Reckless Driving" had panned slightly to the left in the bottom image, the old Hughes Airport would become visible.

# DARBY AVENUE

Located in Reseda, a one block stretch of street was used from Sherman Way south to Gault Street. Very little has changed since "Phony Insurance" was filmed here.

The loading dock of the Grand Central Warehouse at 7115 Darby Avenue has been enclosed.

Dr. R. L. Snow's office is located at 7125 Darby Avenue. The building to the north of it is located at 7131 Darby Avenue. The buildings on Sherman Way and Darby Avenue are still there (see Sherman Way).

**Located in Chatsworth, this street parallels Topanga Canyon Boulevard. Used in "Narcotics".**

*Top:* The ranch located at 9644 De Soto Avenue was on the east side of the street. The ranch buildings were on the SE corner of De Soto Avenue and Superior Street.

*Bottom:* The roadway connected De Soto Avenue and Browns Canyon Road. When the 118 freeway was constructed, De Soto Avenue was rerouted to the west. The current portion of the old road ends south of the freeway. The ranch in the background has been replaced by a school. A reservoir (now photo white top on right side of image) has been installed since "Narcotics" was filmed there.

**This street was the original State Route 118 which ran through the northern portion of the San Fernando Valley and beyond.**

The Cabin Cafe was located at 20852 Devonshire Street in Chatsworth, just east of De Soto Avenue. The Burger King Restaurant now sits where it was located. It was used in "Hired Killer", "Narcotics" (see above), "Revenge" season 3, and "The Search".

*Top:* The Shopping Cart was located at 21360 Devonshire Street ("Fake Cop")
*Middle and Bottom:* Maggi's Italian Kitchen was located at 21629 Devonshire Street ("Safecracker")

*Above:* The F & C Market was located at 21743 Devonshire Street, set back from the street (it would be behind the building with the arched front in the today shot) ("Hitchhiker")

*Left:* This building was located to the west of the market and set closer to the street—21757 Devonshire Street. It was where the white building is in the above now photo ("Hitchhiker")

Elizabeth's Cafe was across the street from the F & C Market at 21754 Devonshire Street.

*Top:* The car is parked in front of the F & C Market. Through the windshield, the building on a diagonal from the market is located at 21800 Devonshire Street. It is still there. ("Hitchhiker")

*Bottom:* The SE corner of the intersection of Devonshire Street, Topanga Canyon Boulevard, and Santa Susana Pass Road. When the 118 freeway was built, the Santa Susana Pass Road was renamed Topanga Canyon Boulevard and the "new" Santa Susana Pass Road did not start until just north of Tulsa Street. Now it begins farther up the road. In the background you can see Town & Country Cafe. It was located on Topanga Canyon Boulevard (see Topanga Canyon Boulevard). ("Safecracker")

The Chatsworth Cleaners at 21824 Devonshire Street is still in business.

Top image: "Hired Killer"
Bottom Two Images: "Fake Cop"

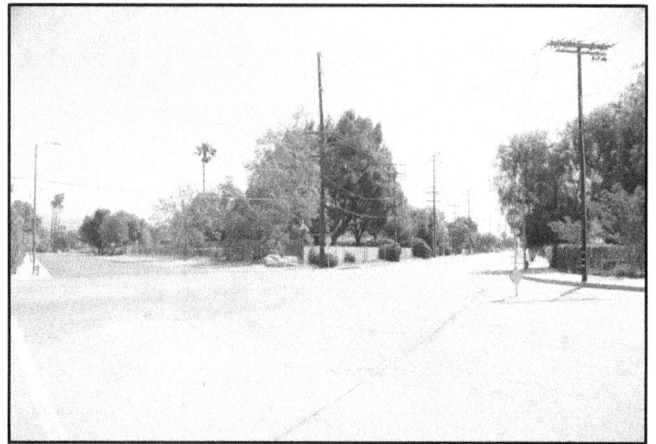

This is the intersection of Devonshire Street and Andora Avenue. Devonshire Street ends a few streets to the west. The house on the NE corner of the intersection appears to still be there, but somewhat remodeled. ("Fake Cop")

130

# DOVER STREET

Located near Glendale in the city of Los Angeles, the house and garage at 3700 Dover Street was used in "Hostage". It is located on the SE corner of Dover Street and Brunswick Avenue.

*Top and left:* The house at 3700 Dover Street has changed little since the late 1950's.

*Bottom:* Across the street at 3701 Dover Street is a duplex which also looks the same. In fact, the entire neighborhood, as seen in the episode, remains the same.

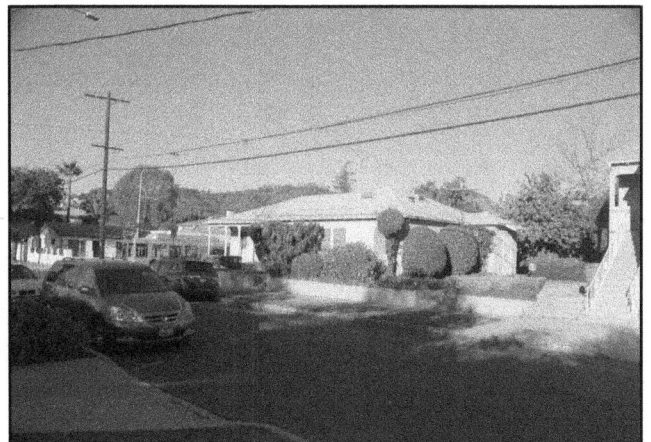

# DUMETZ ROAD

Located in the hills of Woodland Hills, this street was featured in "Gambling" and "Released Convict".

The house above is still there (see right), however, the empty property on the corner now has a residence. This is the intersection of Dumetz Road and Serrania Avenue. ("Gambling)

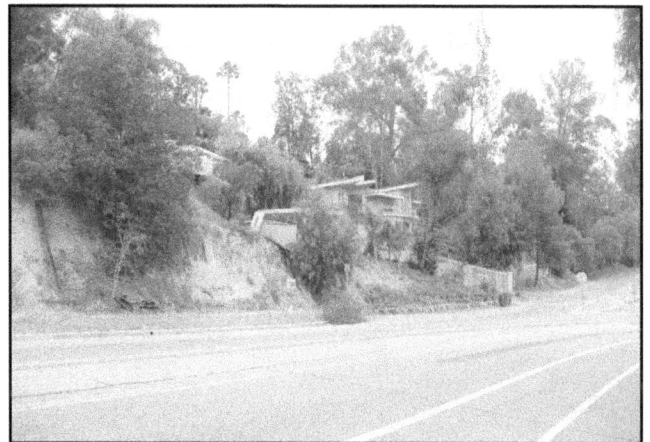

*Top:* Dumetz Road heading east from Ybarra Road ("Released Convict")
*Middle:* Intersection of Dumetz Road and Campo Road ("Released Convict")
*Bottom:* Dumetz Road at Campo Road ("Released Convict")

The fire hydrant in the bottom image on left is hidden by a bush in the now shot on right.

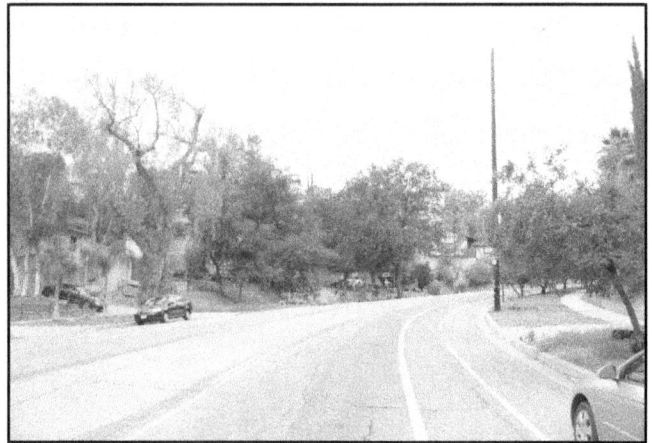

*Top:* The patrol car is parked in front of 21651 Dumetz Road ("Released Convict")
*Above:* The car is traveling on the old Dumetz Road eastbound from Campo Road and Villena Avenue. The street has been subsequently widened. The house on the left is hidden by trees in the right image and has been somewhat modified. ("Released Convict")

# DUPONT STREET

This street, historically, was the closest to the Chatsworth Train Depot. However, the main entrance was from Devonshire Street a quarter-mile to the north along a long unpaved road. This station was used in "Hired Killer" and "Revenge" (season 3).

*Top:* The west side of the station. The now photo has the approximate location of the station drawn in ("Revenge" season 3)
*Above:* The track (east and south) side of the station. Above right is an historical look. ("Revenge" season 3)
*Right:* A 1952 aerial photograph with the station in the oval

Located a block north of Santa Monica Boulevard in Los Angeles, Beverly Glen Boulevard bisects this street. Filming was done in the adjacent blocks for "Portrait of Death".

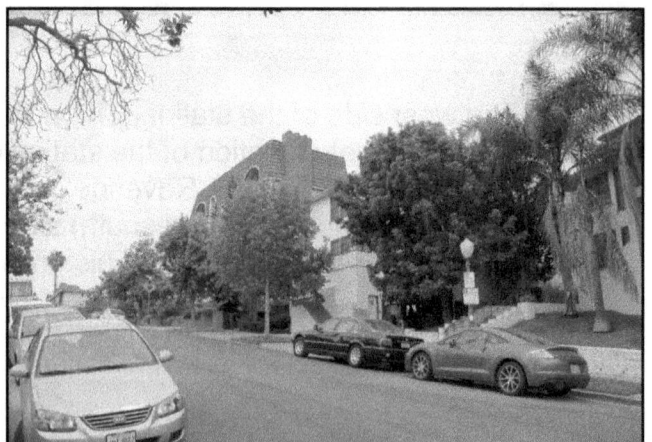

*Top:* Across the street from 10374 Eastborne Avenue
*Middle:* 10403 Eastborne Avenue
*Bottom:* 10407 Eastborne Avenue

## EDDY STREET

This street paralleled along the south side of the Southern Pacific line in Northridge. The Anvil Building Material Co. was located at 18333 Eddy Street, about halfway between Reseda Boulevard and Lindley Avenue, and had a loading dock on the track side. It is seen in the background of a scene in "Train Copter".

Frosty's Day and Night Truck & Auto Service located at 3924 W. El Segundo Boulevard was used for 2 locations: the front end as one and the back end as another.

*Above:* This building is located at 3940 W. El Segundo Boulevard. The side facing Roselle Avenue acted as one location. The working side of the building (see next page) was used as another location.

The businesses located at 3940 and 3944 W. El Segundo Boulevard were used in the above scenes.

The Seers Lumber Company located at 3856 W El Segundo Boulevard was used as a Highway Patrol office in "Car Theft". When the patrol car pulls into the parking area (see top image, looking east), a portion of a building of the Assembly of God church on W 130th Street is seen in the right side of the image. That same building is now hidden by a tall fence which can be seen in the above right image shooting south.

The patrol car parked in front of the building on the bottom left. It was located approximately where the bottom right image was shot.

# EVERETT STREET

Located in the same general area as Alpine Street, Everett Street does not appear in the episode "False Confession". However, the backyards of the two houses located at 960 and 966 Everett Street were used.

*Top left:* Climbing over the fence into the yard at 960 Everett Street. According to the L.A. Co. Assessor, the house in the background has not been remodeled since it was built. However, it does not look like it now.

*Middle:* Backyard at 960 with the side of the house at 966 in the background

*Bottom:* The south side of the house at 960 Everett Street

*Top:* Eveward Road looking south to Bernardo Road
*Middle:* Turning south on Eveward Road from Stever Court
*Bottom:* 5713 Eveward Road. The front of the house has been built outward towards the street.

142

# EXPOSITION PARK

Home to the Memorial Coliseum, Sports Arena, Natural History Museum, California Science Center, Expo Center, California African American Museum, and the Rose Garden. The streets inside the park are now closed to public transportation, but during filming of "Desperate Men", they were open.

The Wallis Annenberg Building/Science Center School
The back entrance above left appears to be gone, but at least one other is still there.

*Top:* California Science Center—left image is the east side, now covered and expanded; right image is the front, facing the Rose Garden
*MIddle:* The SE corner of the Rose Garden
*Bottom:* State Drive looking east towards the Annenberg Building, used as a Hospital in "Desperate Men"

*Top:* State Drive as it curves towards the south. The front of the Natural History Museum of Los Angeles County (the white building) can be seen. This street no longer goes south.

*Bottom:* State Drive as it heads towards Exposition Park Drive and the Los Angeles Memorial Coliseum. This part of State Drive no longer exists. The statue bust of Louis Kosuth has been removed in order to erect the building which houses the Space Shuttle Endeavour. In the episode "Desperate Men", this scene was flipped to put the Coliseum on the right instead of the left. This caused me problems trying to locate the exact site at this location.

# FARRALONE AVENUE
## A north-south street located west of Topanga Canyon Boulevard in Chatsworth.

*Top:* Farralone Avenue heading north from Chatsworth Street ("Fake Cop")
*Middle:* A cabin, now gone, somewhere on the north end of Farralone Avenue ("Fake Cop")
*Bottom:* Near the cabin ("Fake Cop")

The road in the above images is Andora Avenue. However, the house on the right side of the road, its front is on Farralone Avenue, at 10346. Scenes are from "Fake Cop".

*Top:* Patrol car on Topanga Canyon Boulevard heading south as it passes Plummer Street.

*Middle:* The bridge over Santa Susana Pass Wash at Plummer Street. The wash has been rerouted—it had been located at the current Hanna Street.

*Right:* A view of the Peterson Dairy Farm (see next page).

Scenes are from "Mental Patient".

### Peterson Dairy Farm

Walter C. Peterson, owner of Peterson Dairy and Drive-Ins, has been serving the Chatsworth area with fine quality dairy products for eighteen years. Peterson Dairy has four retail drive-in stores which offer milk products produced by their own herd. There is a cash and carry store at the farm for the economically inclined customer and home delivery service is now available. Mr. Peterson invites parents to bring their children to the farm to see the animals.

9409 Farralone Avenue                                        Phone 341-2784

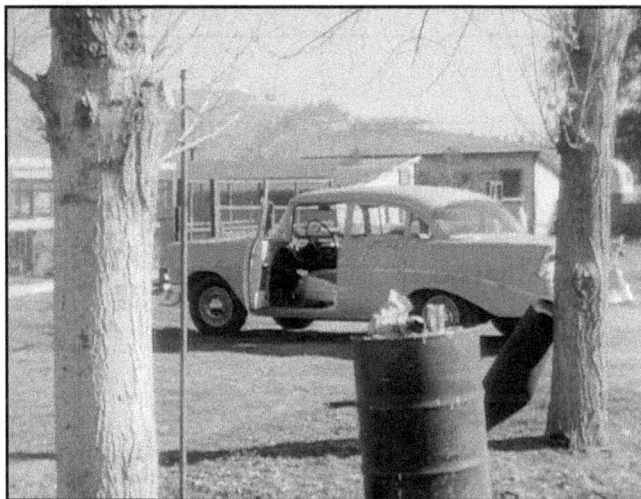

On the left are views of the Peterson Dairy Farm ("Mental Patient"). Top is looking north. Middle is looking northwest. Bottom is also looking northwest. Notice in the last two images the road with the stand of trees along it. Just to the right of that road is the house which you can see in the top image on the previous page. The dairy farm is long gone and the land is now a housing tract. The now images on the right give an overview of where the dairy farm used to be (both views are looking in a southerly direction, the bottom one is Farralone Avenue).

# FERN DELL DRIVE

**Located on the west side of Griffith Park in Western Canyon, Fern Dell is a public fern garden.**

The Trails, located at 2333 Fern Dell Drive, is the current incarnation of this park roadside eatery which was used in two episodes: "Rabies" and "The Trucker".

An area behind and to the side of The Trails (see pages 152 and 153) was used in "Gem Robbery" (season 2), "Hot Dust", "Policewoman", and "Reward".

The east side of Fern Dell Drive is the location of the fern garden. This area is filled with ponds, streams, and plants, especially ferns. In former years, there has been a general neglect to the care of the garden and it has deterioated greatly. This is in the process of changing—the city will be restoring the garden to its past splendor.

A couple of the pools of water were used in "Policewoman" and "Rabies" (see above). Below is one of the current waterless ponds. The garden is about a mile in length and I have not attempted to locate the exact same pools as above.

Garage

Garage

House

The
Trails

FERN DELL DRIVE

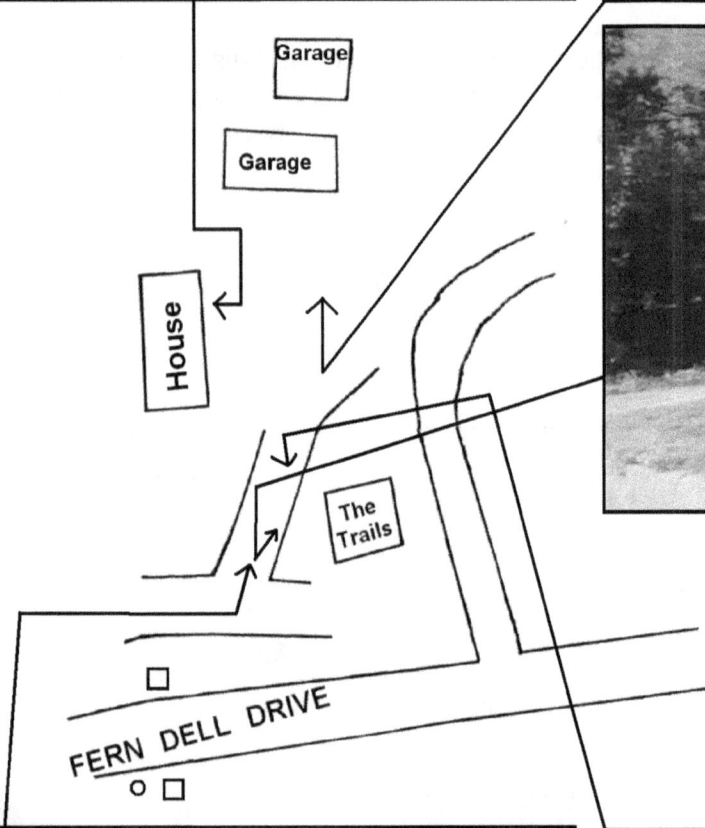

*Left:* The two squares are the half-height posts for the gates. The circle is the lamppost which is seen from the driveway.

*Center:* A 1954 aerial of the location. The parallel white lines show the approximate location of the driveway.
*Right:* The approximate location of the large garage building
*Bottom Left:* Location of the house
*Bottom Right:* Approximate location of the driveway

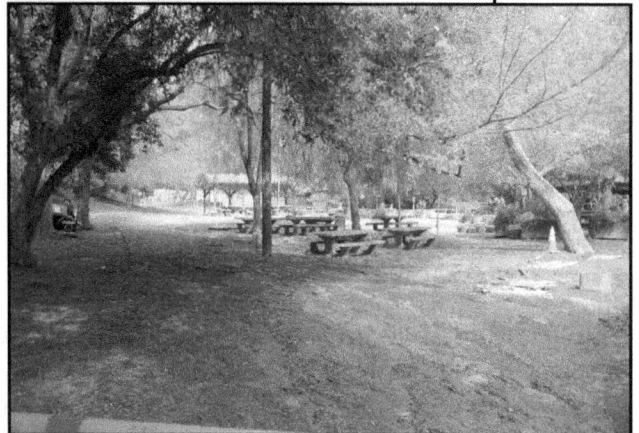

## FIGUEROA TERRACE

This street, originally named Figueroa Street, is west of the 110 freeway. At the freeway, it connects with Figueroa Street. It was used in "False Confession" and "Bank Messenger".

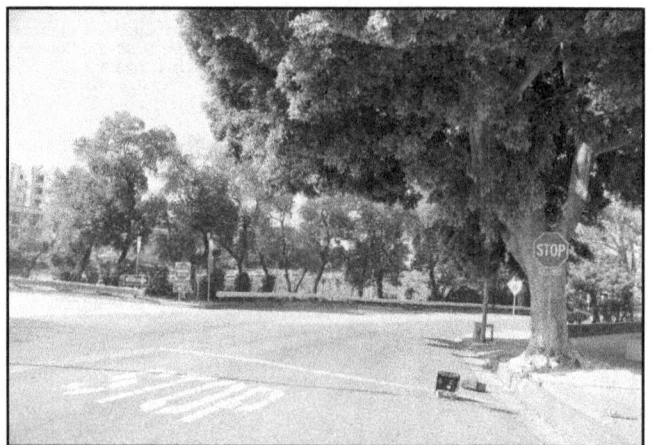

*Top:* Patrol car is at the intersection of Figueroa Terrace and W. College Street
*Middle:* 871 Figueroa Terrace
*Bottom:* Figueroa Terrace and an exit from the 110 freeway

154

**Mayo Motel**
840 N. Figueroa Street
"Bank Messenger"

**Mayo Motel**
840 N. Figueroa Street
"Bank Messenger"

Located in the Los Feliz section of Los Angeles. The street to the west and east of Hillhurst Avenue was used in "Reformation" and "Suspected Cop".

This is the south side of Finley Avenue just east of Hillhurt Avenue. The apartment building (left of the two two-story buildings) is located at 4452 Finley Avenue. The houses on this side of the street, except for a couple farther east and not seen in "Reformation", are long gone, replaced by apartment buildings.

This is Finley Avenue just west of Hillhurst Avenue. While the church still remains at 4510 Finley Avenue, many of the other buildings have changed. Houses have been replaced by apartments. As seen in "Suspected Cop".

# FOOTHILL BOULEVARD

The western stretch of this major road, both north and south of Balboa Boulevard in the city of Sylmar, was used in "Escort". The then new Interstate 5 freeway can be seen in some of the scenes.

*Top:* Just north of Balboa Boulevard
*Center and Bottom:* Near Filbert Street

**A short six block stretch of road crossing Canyon Drive south of Bronson Canyon. A house on the southeast corner of Foothill Drive and Bronson Drive was used in "The Collector".**

# FOREST LAWN DRIVE

Located on the north side of Griffith Park, running from Universal Studios on the west to the 134 freeway on the east, the street was originally named Hollingsworth Drive. It was renamed after the Forest Lawn Cemetary which fronts on a large stretch of this road.

*Top:* Near the entrance to Forest Lawn ("Hitchhiker Dies")
*Bottom:* The west end, Barnham Boulevard in the distance ("Runaway Boy")

**The former United Artists/Goldwyn Studio was located on Formosa Avenue. Across the street to the west was the ZIV Studio where *Highway Patrol* was based.**

*Top and Middle:* 916 N. Formosa Avenue is on the south side of this building ("Hot Cargo")
*Bottom:* The north side is at 920 N. Formosa Avenue ("Hot Cargo"); now view is from opposite direction.

*Top:* The NE corner of Formosa Avenue and Willoughby Avenue ("Hot Cargo")
*Middle:* The NW corner of Formosa Avenue and Willoughby Avenue ("Hot Cargo")
*Bottom:* The SE corner of Formosa Avenue and Romaine Street ("Hot Cargo")

*Top and Bottom:* The storage tank on Formosa Avenue ("Human Bomb")
*Middle:* United Artists Studio facing Formosa Avenue ("Hot Cargo")
*Bottom:* United Artists Studio. The backlot was removed in 1954.

A semi-major roadway south of Griffith Park, running east-west. Three separate locations were used in "Blood Money", "Temptation", and "Transmitter Danger".

*Top:* The Cedars of Lebanon Hospital, 4833 Fountain Avenue ("Blood Money")
*Middle:* Palmers Market at 7714 Fountain Avenue was triangle shaped. One of the Pacific Electric Interurban lines ran diagonally alongside the building ("Transmitter Danger")
*Bottom:* The intersection of Fountain Avenue and Genesee Avenue ("Temptation")

## FRANKLIN AVENUE

An east-west street located just south of Griffith Park. The Bronsonian Pharmacy at 5889 Franklin Avenue was used in "The Collector".

**Franklin Canyon Drive begins at Beverly Drive in the northern reaches of Beverly Hills and heads up into the hills to the Franklin Canyon Reservoir.**

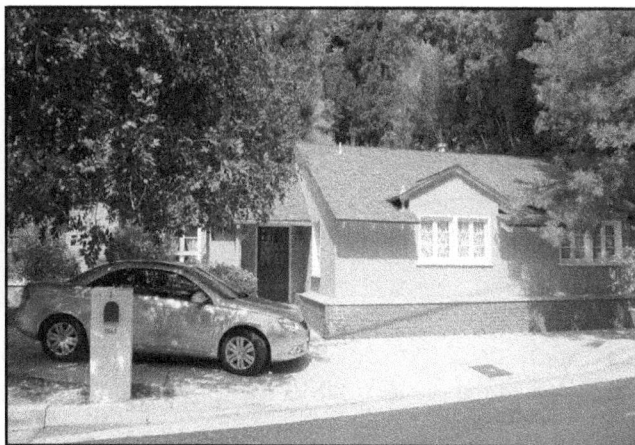

The "Escaped Mental Patient" picked up his "date" at 1845 Franklin Canyon Drive and walked her to his car which was parked in front of 1853 Franklin Canyon Drive.

Originally a part of the Los Angeles Department of Water and Power water supply for Los Angeles, the Upper Franklin Canyon Reservoir has been decommissioned and belongs to the state. The Lower Reservoir is still owned by the DWP.

The lower reservoir was used in "Psycho". It is now decommissioned. A newer reservoir, rubber-lined, was built to the north of it.

The Upper Reservoir, where most filming has taken place, besides *Highway Patrol*, was decommissioned as a water source for Los Angeles. The water level has been lowered since those days to protect the earthen dam. This reservoir and surrounding area, excluding the two houses which were used (see next sections), can be seen in "Breath of a Child", "Escaped Mental Patient, "Fisherman's Luck", "Psycho-Killer", "Revenge" (season 4), and "The Sniper".

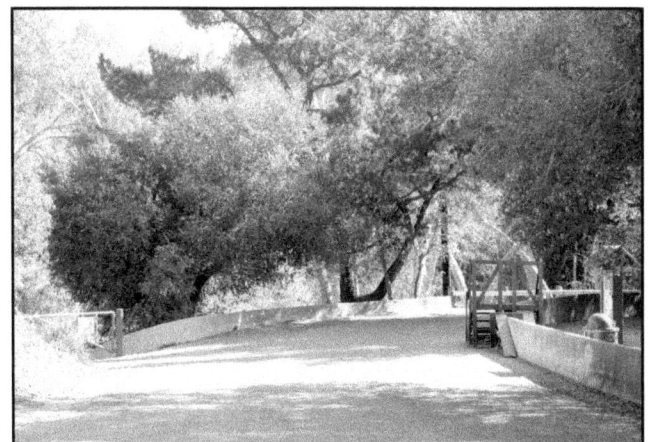

The Dam Keeper's house (the Lower House), was located at the west side of the dam. It can be seen in "Breath of a Child", "Escaped Mental Patient", "Fisherman's Luck", "Psycho-Killer", and "The Sniper".

The gas pumps seen above were a prop used in "Breath of a Child". After filming, they were taken back to the studio ("The Sniper").

The upper house was located near the northern end of the reservoir. Sometime after the state acquired the property, the house was removed. There is now an amphitheater where the house had been. This house can be seen in "Breath of a Child", "Psycho-Killer", "Revenge" (season 4), and "The Sniper".

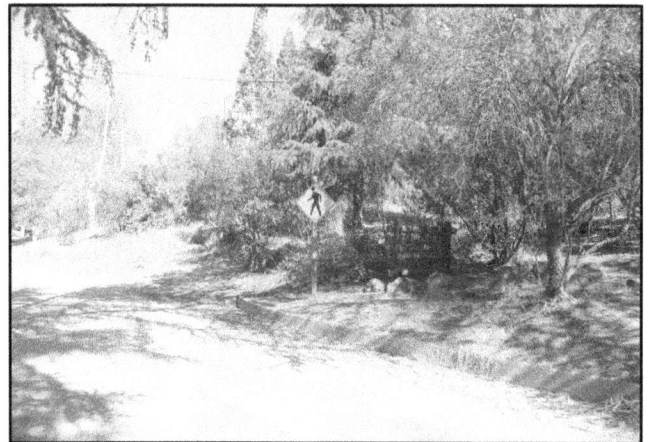

*Top:* "Revenge" (season 4)
*Middle:* "Psycho-Killer"
*Bottom:* "The Sniper"

**This street was the western boundary of the ZIV Studio, running from Santa Monica Boulevard to Romaine Street.**

*Top:* Looking north towards Santa Monica Boulevard ("Girl Bandit")
*Middle:* Looking south towards Romaine Street ("Hitchhiker Dies")
*Bottom:* A side entrance to ZIV Studios ("Careless Cop")

*Top:* 1011 N. Fuller Avenue. It was the Research Craft Plastics Corp when "Prospector",
"Scared Cop", and "Suicide" filmed there. It is now Smashbox Studios.
*Middle and Bottom:* Located just to the north of 1011, the building is now gone, replaced by
a parking lot for Smashbox Studios.

The house at 1729 Gardena Avenue was used in "Express Delivery" and "Gem Robbery" (season 4).

This house was on the NE corner of Gardena Avenue and Mira Loma Avenue.

Three areas along this street in Los Angeles were used in "Explosives", "Gambling Story", and "Temptation".

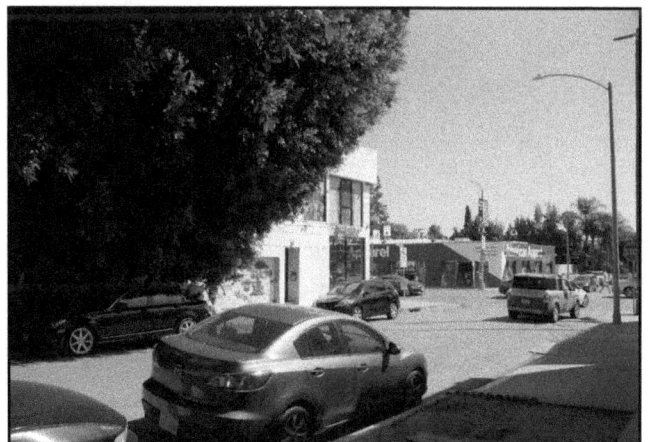

*Top:* 1309 N Genesee Avenue ("Temptation")
*Middle:* 1609 N Genesee Avenue ("Explosives")
*Bottom:* NE corner N Genesee Avenue and Melrose Avenue ("Gambling Story")

*Top:* NW corner of N. Genesee Avenue and Melrose Avenue ("Gambling Story")
*Middle:* The house in the background with the rectangular chimney is located at 715 N. Genesee Avenue ("Gambling Story")
*Bottom:* The house in the background with the brick chimney is located at 721 N. Genesee Avenue ("Gambling Story")

## GLENDALE BOULEVARD

**Located just south of Glendale and east of the Los Angeles River, "Hostage" used two areas along this street.**

*Top:* The Safeway market was locate at 3080 Glendale Boulevard on the right half of the current gas station property.

*Middle and Bottom:* 3010 and 3012 were located next door to the Club Tee Yee (3208). 3010 has been combined with 3012 and is now Gebhardt's Dry Cleaning.

## GOODLAND AVENUE
**Located in Studio City north of the Los Angeles River, "Split Robbery" used a two block stretch between Bloomfield Street on the north and Valleyheart Drive on the south.**

*Top:* 4242 Goodland Avenue
*Middle:* Looking south from 4242 Goodland Avenue
*Bottom:* 4320 Goodland Avenue

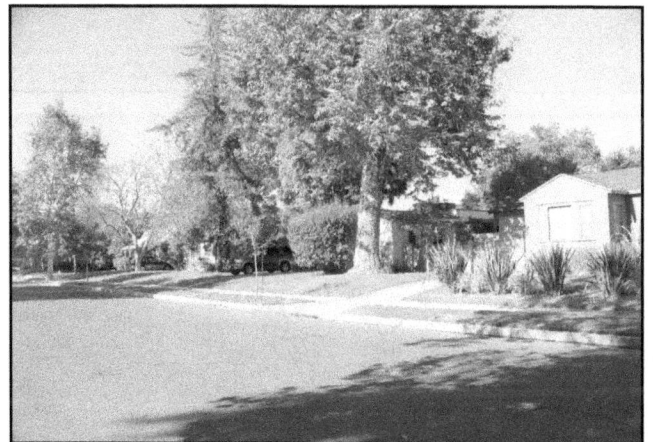

*Top:* Looking north from 4320 Goodland Avenue towards Bloomfield Street
*Middle:* Looking south from 4320 Goodland Avenue
*Bottom:* The west side of the street looking southward from 4320 Goodland Avenue

**Located directly north of the ZIV Studio, it was a dead end street. Used in the "Hitchhiker Dies" episode.**

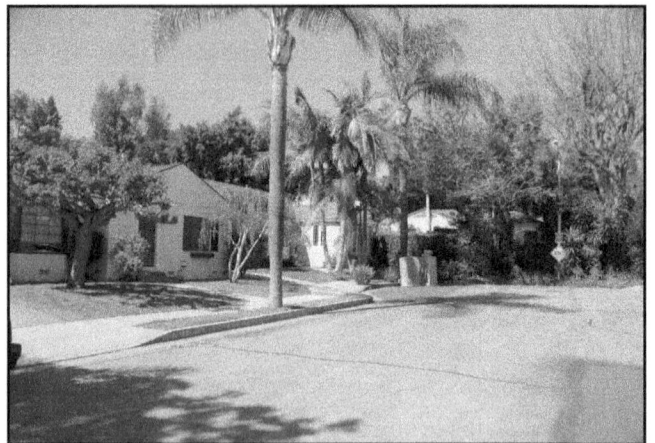

The house was located at 1233 Greenacre Avenue. In the bottom left image, all three buildings are still there, although the apartment building behind is now covered by foliage from the Greenacre side.

# GRESHAM STREET

The building used as a motel in "Confession" is next door to the oldest church in Northridge. When the episode was filmed, the building was only one story. It now has a second story. The buildings across the street seen in the episode are still there, though partly hidden by a newer building.

The church is located at 18531 Gresham Street, just west of Reseda Boulevard.

# GRIFFITH PARK

One of the largest parks in any city at over 4,000 acres. It is home to The Observatory, the Greek Theater, a zoo, Fern Dell, Traveltown, and 2 golf courses, among other park amenities. From the time of filming to today, the zoo has moved and several roads have been removed or rerouted.

The parking lot and grounds of the Pony Ride were used in "Convict's Wife"

The Coolidge Golf Course is now the Tregnan Golf Academy.

*Top:* Heading to Coolidge from Crystal Springs Road ("Convict's Wife").
*Middle:* Griffith Park Boulevard just north of the entrance to Coolidge ("Reformation").
*Bottom:* Griffith Park Boulevard just north of the entrance to Coolidge ("Cargo Hi Jack").

A turnaround for Crystal Springs Road (lower) and Griffith Park Boulevard (upper) a little ways north of the minature train ride ("Reformation"). Nowadays, there is an entrance and exit from the adjacent 5 freeway at the right.

The snack shack (top) was near the tennis courts. The building (middle) is a bathroom. The road (bottom) heading towards the Park Center Snack Shop building (see next page). The roads in this area were removed for additional parking for the Old Zoo. Scenes are from "Reformation".

The old snack shop at the park. Scenes are from "Convict's Wife".

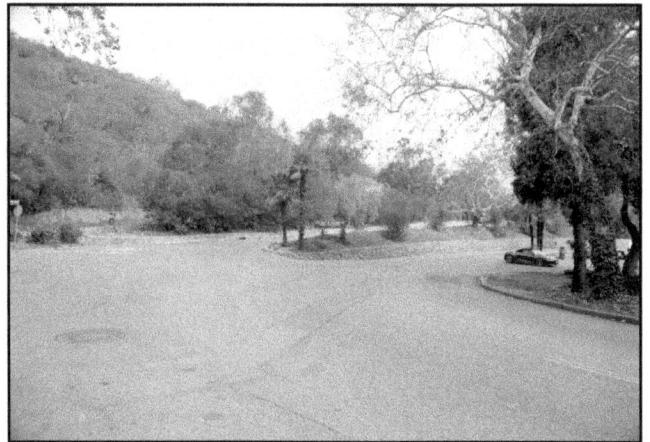

Griffith Park Camp is a boy's camp (the girls have one in Bronson Canyon). Seen here in "Rabies" is the entrance to the camp.

A 1954 aerial of the Boy's Camp. The 5-sided outline is the main building. The rectangle shows the location of the tennis court. The oval is the large mountain cabin. The X shows the start of the stairway up to the small cabin. The camp was used in "Amnesia", "Dan's Vacation", "Mountain-Copter", "Rabies", and "Reformation".

This was the main building at the camp in the 1950's. It no longer exists. An amphitheater now sits here. Top image is from "Amnesia"; the lower image is from "Dan's Vacation".

*Top:* A front view of the main building ("Rabies"). At the top middle right you can just see the large cabin seen more fully in the lower image ("Mountain-Copter").

*Top:* The tennis courts near the main building ("Reformation").
*Middle:* The stairs to the small cabin are in the background ("Amnesia") and a better view on the right from an historical photo from 1955.
*Bottom:* The small cabin ("Mountain-Copter"). A portion of the far side can be seen on the right from an historical photo from 1955.

**Located in a residential area of West Hollywood, south of Fountain Avenue and east of Genesee Avenue. Used in "Transmitter Danger".**

The apartment building at 7733 Hampton Avenue was used in this episode. The apartment building to its right (east) side at 7719 can be seen. Both buildings have changed little since filming was done there.

**Located in the Santa Monica Mountains between Laurel Canyon Boulevard and Nichols Canyon Road, this is a short street used in "Killer on the Run".**

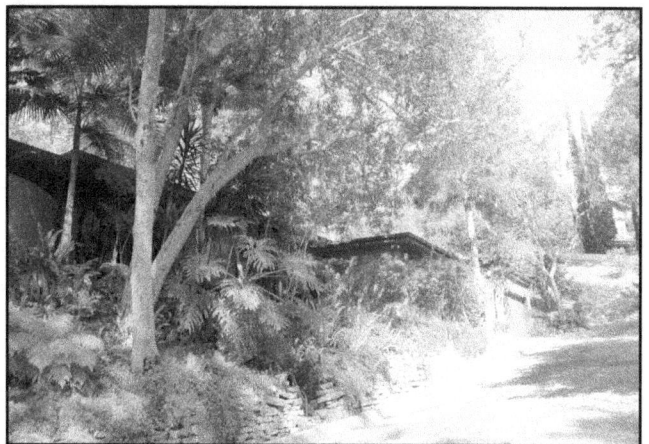

*Top:* The northern end of Harlesden Court before it turns to the right for a short ways. What appears to be a roadway going uphill is a driveway to a house out-of-sight to the left.
*Bottom:* Looking south from the house at 2615 Harlesden Court. The now photo shows the house, but the view is looking up (north) the street.

Located in the city of Lawndale, Hawthorne Boulevard is a major north-south street. A building at 15603 Hawthorne Boulevard, at the SW corner with 156th Street, was used in "Lookout".

At the time of filming, this stretch of road through Agoura and Calabasas was a newly opened 4-lane separated highway (2 lanes each way). When the highway was converted into a freeway and widened, some of the exits for the highway disappeared.

The area of Highway 101 used for the episode "Road-Block" and appeared in the opening credits of each episode was located several hundred yards east of the Palo Comado Canyon Road bridge.

The patrol cars on the highway on the facing page are on the southbound side of the road (the lower of the two above) and a few hunded left west (to the left) of the exit. That exit was removed when the highway was converted to a freeway. To the right is a now image of the end of the exit where it connected with Calabasas Road (at the current Calle Montecillo).

# HILLCREST STREET

**Located on the northwest side of El Segundo, just south of the Los Angeles International Airport (LAX). Used in "Lookout".**

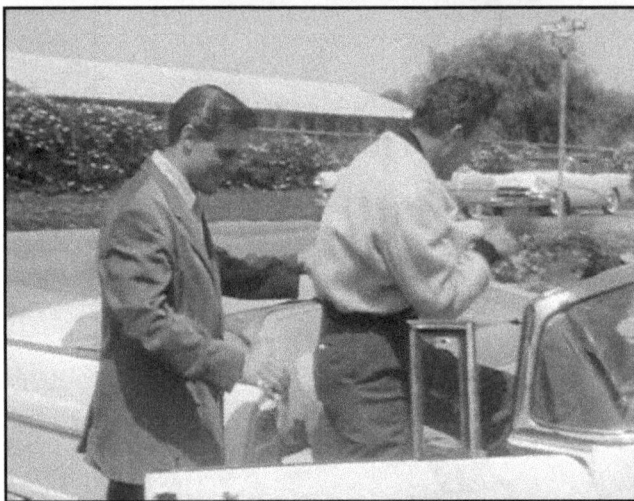

The house was located at 854 Hillcrest Street on the SE corner with Walnut Avenue. For many years, there was a playfield with baseball diamond across the street. There was also a building which looked similar to the backside of a school. However, I have not found any data on what that building was. That entire side of the street (west) is now subdivided into housing (sometime between 1972 and 1980).

# HILLHURST AVENUE

Located in East Hollywood and running from Hollywood Boulevard north into Griffith Park. Episodes filmed there were "Bank Messenger", "Dead Hunter", "Double Death", "Framed Cop", "Reformation", and "Suspected Cop".

Used in "Double Death", 1662 Hillhurst Aveue stood in as Highway Patrol headquarters. The top two images show its HP use. The bottom image shows the building from a short distance to the north.

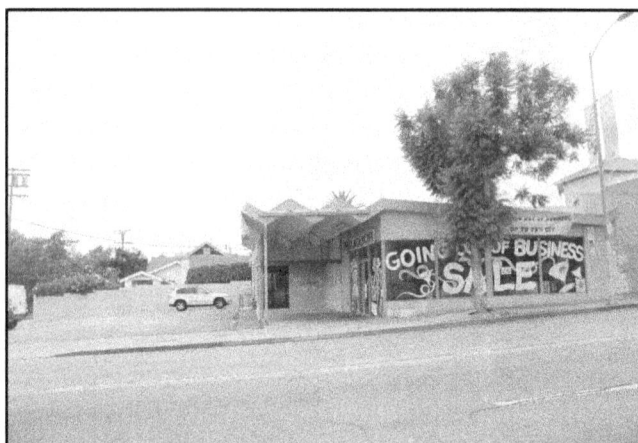

*Top:* Ise's Automotive Service, 1774 N. Hillhurst Avenue ("Double Death")
*Middle:* Apartment building, 1822 N. Hillhurst Avenue ("Double Death")
*Bottom:* E. D. Cristman Real Estate, 1863 N. Hillhurst Avenue ("Double Death")

*Top:* Union Oil Service Station, 2000 Hillhurst Avenue ("Suspected Cop")
*Middle:* Hillhurst Mart, 2060 Hillhurst Avenue ("Double Death")
*Bottom:* Hillhurst Variety Store, 2068 Hillhurst Avenue ("Suspected Cop")

Used as a bank in "Bank Messenger", this was the Brownie Letter Shop, 1751 Hillhurst Avenue.

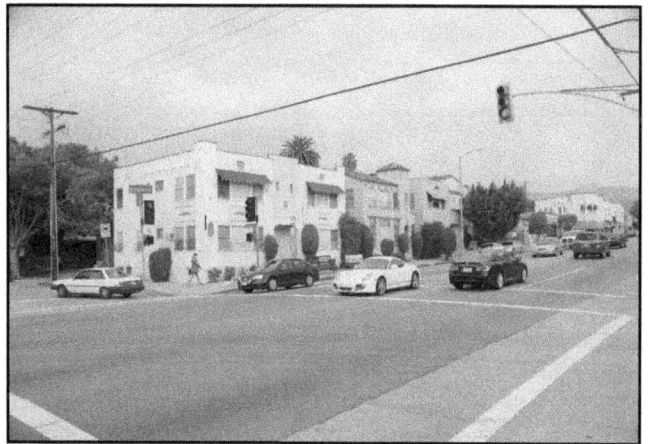

*Top:* Across the street from 1751 Hillhurst Avenue on the NE corner with Kingswell Avenue, the official street address of the house was 4457 Kingswell Avenue ("Bank Messenger")
*Middle:* Department of Water and Power, 1675 Hillhurst Avenue ("Double Death")
*Bottom:* Apartment building to the north of the DWP building on the NW corner of Prospect Avenue, 1701 Hillhurst Avenue ("Dead Hunter")

*Top:* Apartment, 1720 Hillhurst Avenue ("Reformation")
*Middle:* House, 1714 Hillhurst Avenue ("Reformation")
*Bottom:* The house in the background left is at 1714 Hillhurst Avenue. The house behind the male actor's head was located at 4500 Kingswell Avenue (SW corner with Hillhurst Avenue) ("Bank Messenger")

Price Street makes a T intersection with Hillhurst Avenue. In "Framed Cop", the buildings to the north and south along HIllhurst Avenue, as well as on Price Street, were used.

*Top:* To the north of Price Street
*Middle:* To the south of Price Street
*Bottom:* The SE corner of Price Street and Hillhurst Avenue

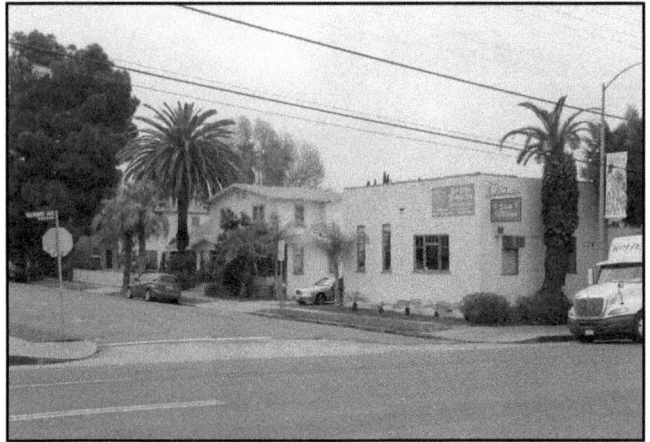

More views of the Hillhurst Avenue/Price Street intersection

Top: "Double Death"
Bottom: "Framed Cop"

209

*Top:* Arriving near Jebs Instruments, 4641 Hollywood Boulevard
*Middle:* Heading east on Hollywood Boulevard from Vermont Avenue, passing the Atlantic Richfield (now Shell) gas station
*Bottom:* Traveling pass the Colt Ventilation of America building, 4652 Hollywood Boulevard

*Top:* Furniture Store at 907 N. Hollywood Way
*Middle:* Kirk's Drug Store, 817 N. Hollywood Way
*Bottom:* Alley on south side of Kirk's Drug Store

**Located south of Santa Monica Boulevard and west of Beverly Glen Boulevard. Used in "Portrait of Death".**

The car of the killer is parked on Holmby Avenue, south of Santa Monica Boulevard. The 2-story building in the top image actually faces Santa Monica Boulevard (10460). The wood shingled 2-story building in the bottom image is located at 1812 Holmby Avenue.

# IBANEZ AVENUE
A short stretch of this road, which runs on the north side of the Woodland Hills Country Club, was used in "Gambling".

*Top:* The Flight View Restaurant, 310 E. Imperial Avenue, was used in "Reckless Driving" ("Lookout")

*Middle:* A former motel, 548 W. Imperial Avenue ("Lookout")

*Bottom:* The 600 block of W. Imperial Avenue ("Lookout")

A major east-west road from the ocean to Riverside County. The section located next to Los Angeles International Airport was used in "Reckless Driving".

**Located in Culver City on the south side of Ballona Creek, the 9400 block was used in "Radioactive". Adjacent to Jefferson Boulevard on the south side are the Baldwin Hills Oil Fields, used in "Oil Lease".**

*Top:* 9450 Jefferson Boulevard
*Middle:* 9425 Jefferson Boulevard
*Bottom:* 9405 Jefferson Boulevard

The Baldwin Hills Oil Fields are still active and are closed to the public. The now shots above are generic ones of the location and not specifically related to the then images shown above from "Oil Lease".

**Located in the Los Feliz section of East Hollywood, a section to the east of Hillhurst Avenue was used in "Reformation".**

*Top:* Apartments, 4451 Kingswell Avenue

*Bottom:* Heading east from 4451 Kingswell Avenue. Apartments on right are located at 4444-4450 Kingswell Avenue.

Unrelated to our *Highway Patrol* location journey, just down Kingswell Avenue from this location, at 4506 was located the first studio in California of Walt Disney, in a garage. His second studio was also on Kingswell Avenue on the west end of the street.

Located at 12024 Balboa Boulevard in Granada Hills, the golf course opened in 1957. It was used extensively in "The 7th Green".

*Top:* The gardener/landscaper's building was located in the oval in the above map. The original building seen in "The 7th Green" is either gone or moved. The current building in the oval is to the west of the original site.

## LAKESIDE DRIVE
This street is only one block in length, located west of Warner Bros Studios in Burbank. Used in "Hitchhiker Dies". Apartments are at 4439 Lakeside Drive.

# LARCHMONT BOULEVARD

This street runs through Larchmont Village, a small two-block shopping district in Los Angeles.

*Top:* Wilshire Studios, 103 N. Larchmont Boulevard, side entrance ("Counterfeit")
*Middle:* Heading south towards 1st Street ("Counterfeit")
*Bottom:* Landis Department Store, 157 N. Larchmonth Boulevard ("Counterfeit")

*Top:* McCarthy Gift Shop, 161 N. Larchmont Boulevard ("Counterfeit")
*Middle:* Harper Method Approved Shop, 143 N. Larchmont Boulevard ("Counterfeit")
*Bottom:* Larchmont Travel Agency, 221 N. Larchmont Boulevard ("Chain Store")

The Wilshire Food Center at 214 N. Larchmont Boulevard
("Chain Store")

The Earl Hays Press, 1121 N. Las Palmas Avenue
("Counterfeit")

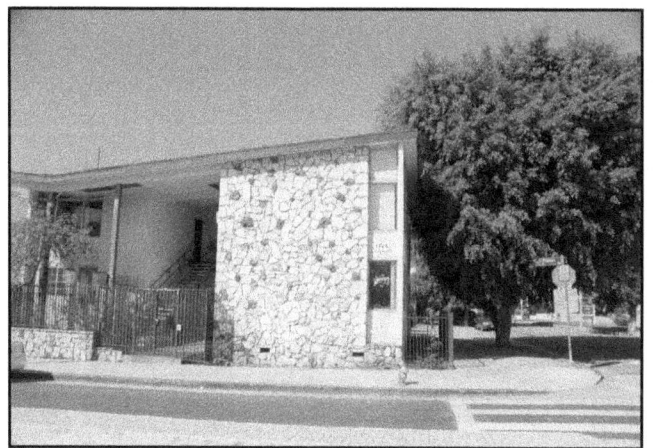

*Top:* The Las Palmas Hotel, 1738 N. Las Palmas Avenue on left, First Baptist Church on Hollywood Boulevard in the distance ("Released Convict")
*Middle and Bottom:* Two views of the apartments at 1749 N. Las Palmas Avenue ("Released Convict")

*Top:* The apartment building on the NE corner of Las Palmas Avenue and Yucca Street is now a playground for the Yucca Community Center ("Released Convict")
*Bottom:* The telephone booths on the SE corner of Las Palmas Avenue and Yucca Street, now the Yucca Street Mini Park ("Released Convict")

The 4400 block of Lexington Avenue, just east of Virgil Avenue, was used in "Convicted Innocent".

*Top:* House at 4457 Lexington Avenue was recently torn down
*Middle:* House at 4455 Lexington Avenue is still there
*Bottom:* House at 4453 Lexington Avenue is still there

**Located just west of Dodger Stadium, a portion of the original Lilac Place was removed when Elysian Park Avenue was extended into Dodger Stadium.**

While the house at 1233 Lilac Place still remains, sitting all alone, the apartment house next door was removed when Elysian Park Avenue was extended beyond Lilac Place for an entrance into Dodger Stadium. The apartment house apparently fronted on Elysian Park Avenue.

*Top:* House, 1233 Lilac Place ("The Judge")
*Bottom:* Apartment House, next door (right of) to 1233 Lilac Place ("The Judge")

*Top:* 1232Lilac Place ("Foster Child")
*Bottom:* 1226 Lilac Place ("Foster Child")

**Except for a truncted western end, this street stills remains mostly intact from pre-Dodger Stadium days.**

Originally a Navy Reserve Center, it is now the property of the Los Angeles City Fire Department (see top images—the building in the background).

*Top:* From "Hitch Hiker"
*Bottom:* From "The Judge"

*Top:* House, 3755 Longridge Avenue ("Expose")
*Middle:* House, 3777 Longridge Avenue ("Expose")
*Bottom:* House, 3655 Longridge Avenue ("Expose")

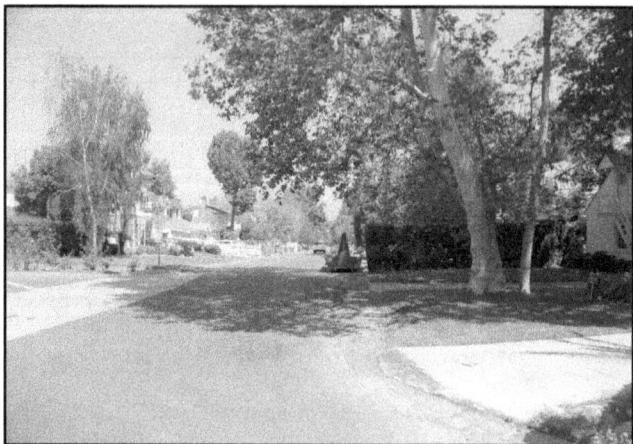

A traveling shot from Longridge Avenue southbound onto Ethel Avenue northbound ("Expose").

**A major east-west street in Los Angeles and Glendale. Used in three episodes: "Express Delivery", "Framed Cop", and "Gem Robbery" (season 4).**

*Top:* The Maple Shop, 206 W. Los Feliz Boulevard ("Gem Robbery" season 4)
*Middle:* The Tam O'Shanter parking lot, 2980 Los Feliz Boulevard ("Framed Cop")
*Bottom:* The Los Feliz Hotel, 3101 Ls Feliz Boulevard ("Framed Cop")

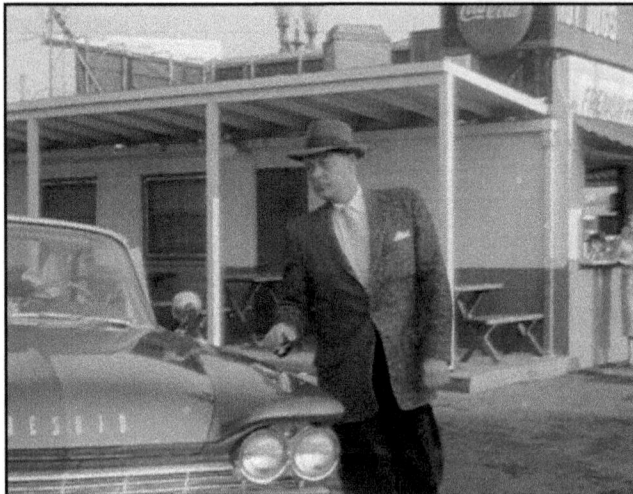

*Top:* "A" shaped roof, 3126 Los Feliz Boulevard ("Framed Cop")
*Middle and Bottom:* Parking lot behind Hot Dog stand, NE corner Los Feliz Boulevard and San Fernando Road ("Framed Cop")

The gateway into the apartment complex at 4150 Los Feliz Boulevard (seen in above now photo) and the interior courtyard were both used in the episode "Framed Cop". However, I took no now photos of those areas.

*Top and Middle:* The intersection of Los Feliz Boulevard and Perlita Avenue ("Framed Cop")
*Bottom:* Apartment building, 4150 Los Feliz Boulevard ("Framed Cop")

238

# MAGNOLIA BOULEVARD

A nursery located in Sherman Oaks at 12920 Magnolia Boulevard was used in "Phony Cop".

Located south of Los Angeles International Airport, the main business district in El Segundo is along Main Street. Used in "Reckless Driving".

*Top:* 520 Main Street
*Middle:* United Methodist Church, in background, 540 Main Street
*Bottom:* Building across the street, 519-525 Main Street

*Top:* 24346 Main Street
*Middle:* 24358 Main Street
*Bottom:* 24355 Main Street

The Soledad Hotel and Cafe were located at 24367 Main Street. The Cocktail Lounge was located at 24371 Main Street. The office of Paul Palmer, Attorney, was located at 24369 Main Street.

243

*Top:* 901 N. Martel Avenue
*Bottom:* 857 N. Martel Avenue

The intersection of Medio Drive and Sunset Boulevard was used in "The Christmas Story".

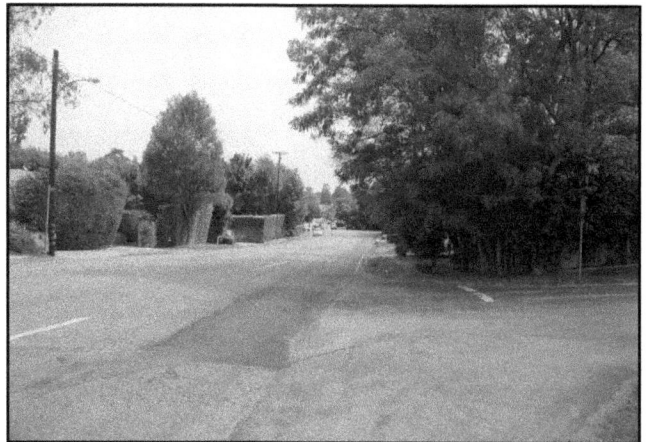

*Top:* House, 104 S. Medio Drive
*Bottom:* Traveling east on Sunset Boulevard after leaving Medio Drive

**MELROSE AVENUE**
A major east-west street in Los Angeles. The Fairfax district was used in "Counterfeit",
"Dead Patrolman", "Gambling Story", and "Killer on the Run".

*Top:* William C Jagy Service Station, 7253 Melrose Avenue ("Killer on the Run")
*Middle:* Gene's Auto Works, 7229 Melrose Avenue ("Killer on the Run")
*Bottom:* Nielsen's Books, 7308 Melrose Avenue ("Dead Patrolman")

The Alley behind Nielsen's Books, 7308 Melrose Avenue ("Dead Patrolman")

*Top:* 7326 Melrose Avenue ("Dead Patrolman")
*Middle:* 7327 Melrose Avenue ("Dead Patrolman")
*Bottom:* 7710 Melrose Avenue ("Gambling Story")

*Top:* 7701 Melrose Avenue ("Gambling Story")
*Middle:* Alley behind 7701 Melrose Avenue ("Gambling Story")
*Bottom:* Atlas Heating, 7673 Melrose Avenue ("Gambling Story")

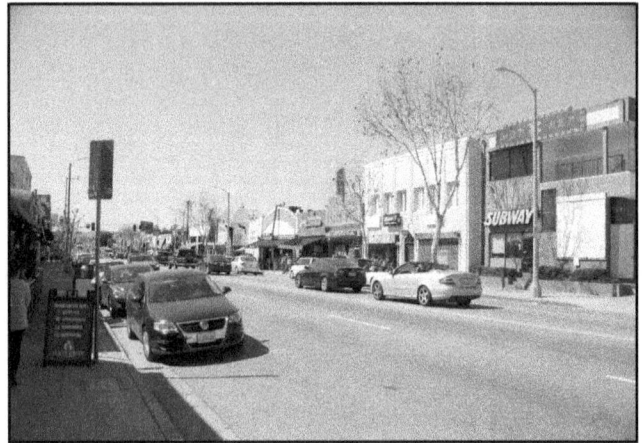

*Top and Middle:* Melrose Market, 7355 Melrose Avenue ("Counterfeit")
*Bottom:* Novelty Quilting, 7373 Melrose Avenue ("Dead Patrolman")

250

**Located in Sherman Oaks. "Expose" used an apartment building at 14065 while "Split Robbery" has a view of an apartment building at 14047.**

In the bottom image, in the distance behind the supermarket, both the apartments at 14065 and 14047 Moorpark Street can be seen.

## MULHOLLAND DRIVE

A 21-mile long road which mostly follows the ridgeline of the Santa Monica Mountains from the Cahuenga Pass to Encino Hills Road. From there, it is a dirt road, closed to vehicles. It ends in Woodland Hills. Episodes filmed along the roadway are "Auto Press", "Explosives", "Hostage-Copter, "Killers on the Run", "Magazine Writer", "Mexican Chase", "Mistaken Identity", "Motorcycle" (season 2), "Officer's Wife", "Oil Lease", "Slain Cabby", and "Trojan Horse". This list does not include those episodes which filmed at the old Fire Station 109 (see next section) on Mulholland Drive.

*Top:* Mulholland Drive at Encino Hills Drive ("Hostage-Copter")
*Bottom:* Mulholland Drive at Roscomare Road, then image looking west along Mulholland Drive, now image looking south at Roscomare Road ("Auto Press")

**Mulholland Drive and Bowmont Drive**

*Top:* Mulholland Drive looking west at Bowmont Drive ("Slain Cabby")
*Middle and Bottom:* Bowmont Drive house ("Trojan Horse")

253

**Mulholland Drive and Franklin Canyon Drive**

*Top and Bottom:* Driving west on Mulholland Drive through the intersection with Franklin Canyon Drive on the left and Coldwater Canyon Avenue on the right ("Mistaken Identity")
*Bottom:* An open space alongside Mulholland Drive just east of Franklin Canyon Drive, now protected from Mulholland Drive by trees ("Mistaken Identity")

**Mulholland Drive and Torreyson Drive**

*Top:* Torreyson Drive at Mulholland Drive ("Killer on the Run")
*Middle:* Torreyson Drive at Mulholland Drive ("Explosives")
*Bottom:* Mulholland Drive heading east from Torreyson Drive ("Killer on the Run")

**Mulholland Drive and Runyon Canyon Road**

*Top and Middle:* Views of the entrances to Runyon Canyon Park ("Officer's Wife")
*Bottom:* Heading west on Mulholland Drive as seen from Runyon Cayon Park entrance.
The Hollywood sign is just visible in the distance ("Officer's Wife").
NOTE: I failed to photograph this angle for the book.

**15341 Mulholland Drive**

"Motorcycle" (season 2)

# 1952 AERIAL MULHOLLAND DRIVE

15433 Mulholland Drive          15341 Mulholland Drive

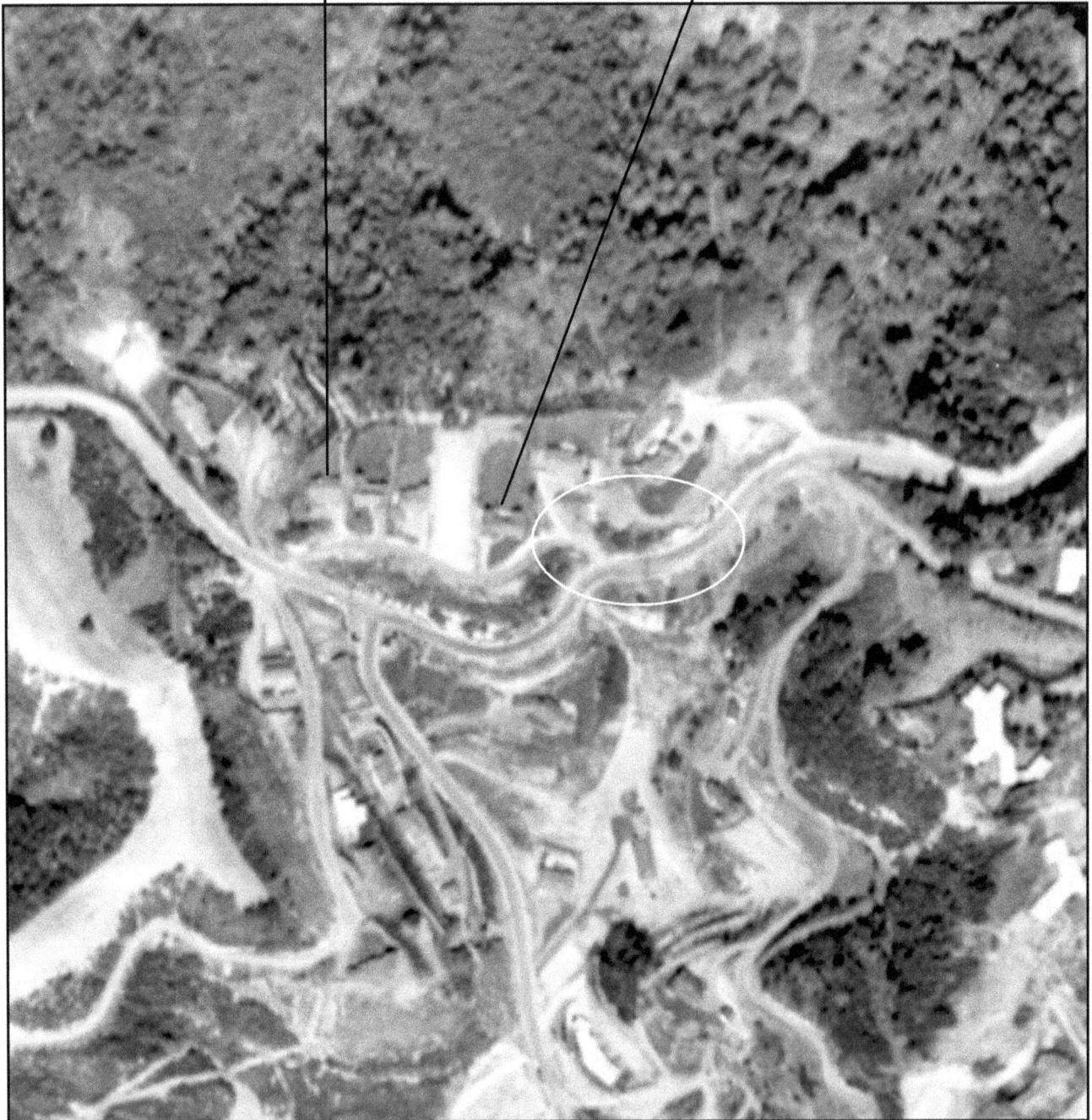

**Mulholland Drive Before Realignment**

This 1952 aerial shows the alignment of Mulholland Drive during the filming days for "Magazine Writer" and "Motorcycle" (season 2). In the 1960's, the roadway was realigned to its present route.

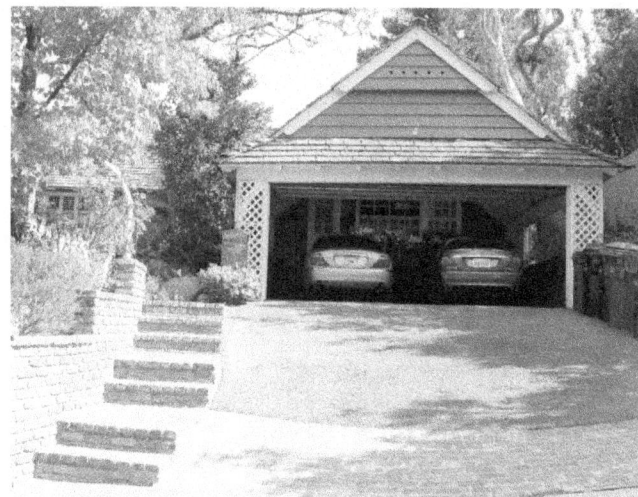

*Left:* This scene corresponds to the white oval in the aerial on the facing age.

## Mulholland Drive Bypass Residential Road

On the north side of Mulholland Drive, east of the Sepulveda Pass, is a residential bypass road where six homes now reside. Both "Magazine Writer" and "Motorcycle" (season 2) use homes on this street. *Above:* the house identified as 15433 is probably now 15411. It is the left-most house of 3 and can be seen on the aerial on the facing page.

**Mulholland Drive West of Fire Station 109**

Fire Station 109 is located at 16500 Mulholland Drive

*Top Images:* Heading west on Mulholland Drive to the dirt turnout on the north side of the street ("Hired Killer")

**The Groves Overlook**

This overlook is across the street from the old fire station location (see next section).
*Top and Middle:* "Mexican Chase"
*Bottom:* "Diversion Robbery"

Located west of the Sepulveda Pass at 16500 Mulholland Drive, the Mountain Patrol 2 station was used in nineteen episodes. In the early 1970's, a regular fire station was erected due west of this patrol station. This station housed mountain firefighting equipment such as bulldozers. A heliocopter pad was built after Fire Station 109 was built and some of the back area of the property has been regraded from when *Highway Patrol* filmed there.

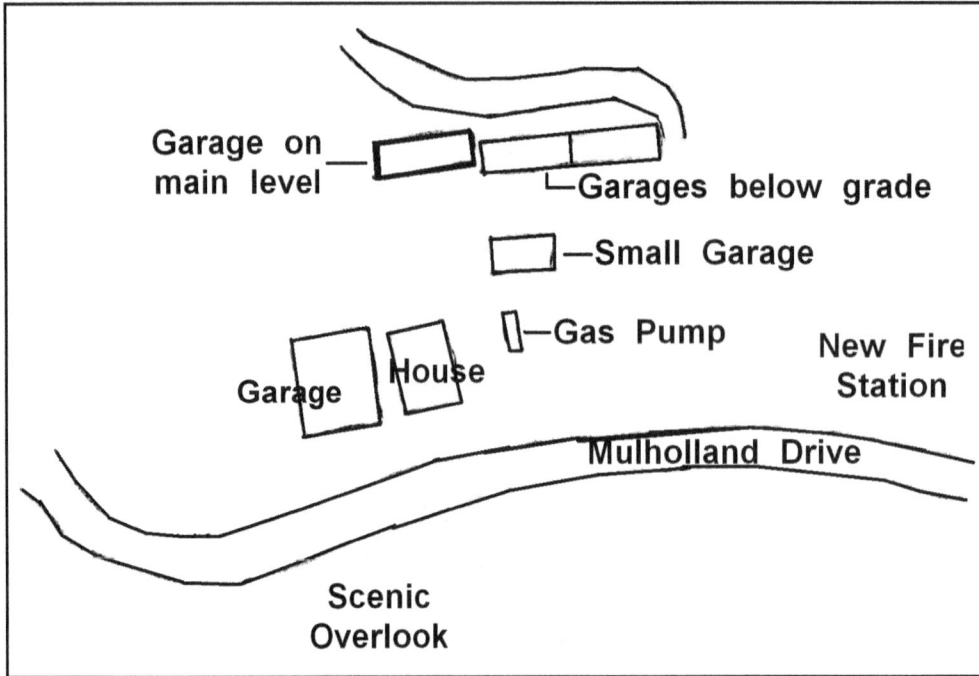

Garage on main level

Garages below grade

Small Garage

Gas Pump

New Fire Station

Garage

House

Mulholland Drive

Scenic Overlook

*Above:* A layout drawing of the site
*Below:* A 1952 aerial of the site

**The Large Garage**

This is the large garage which held the fire fighting equipment. It was located to the east (left) of the house (see map on facing page) and faced north on Mulholland Drive.
*Left:* "Motorcycle" (season 2)
*Right:* "Witness Wife"

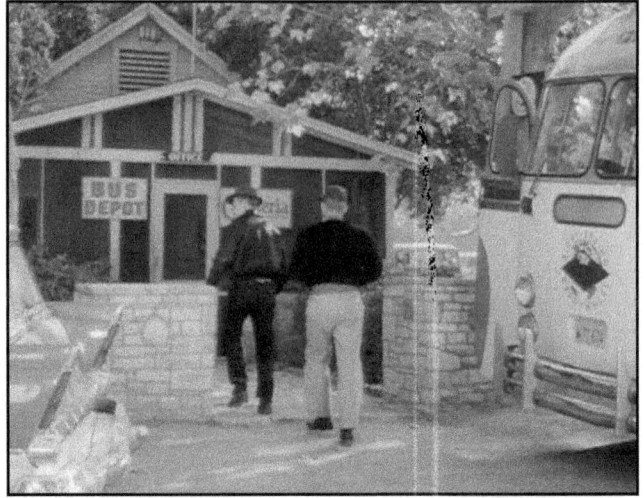

## The House

This building also faced Mulholland Drive. It probably contained the living and dining quarters for the firemen stationed there. The front stone work still remains and the cement pad of the building, but the house is long gone.

*Left:* "Tear Gas Copter"
*Right:* "Migrant Workers"

## The House

This is the west side of the house, facing the parking area.
*Left:* "Motorcycle" (season 2)
*Right:* "Hot Cargo"

## The House

This is the rear of the house and walkway to the parking area.
*Left:* "Tear Gas Copter"
*Right:* "Nitro"

## The Gas Pump and Garage

The gas pump and garage are gone. In the now photo below, the gas pump above was where the tree and garbage can is. The current building is sitting in about the same place as the original one. However, the area behind has been greatly changed—there is a small hill with houses on top, while in the filming days, the area was below grade with 2 buildings (see next section), and a sloping area behind with a road.

*Above left:* "Copter Cave In". *Above right:* "Nitro".

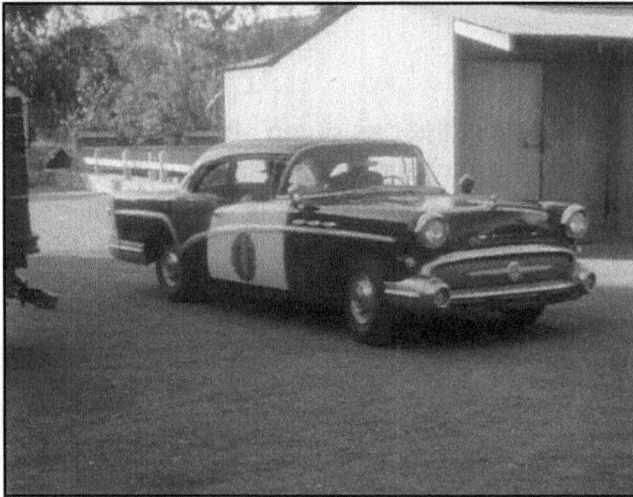

*Above Left:* "Mexican Chase"
*Above Right:* "Hot Cargo"
*Left:* "Nitro"

The top two images show the below grade area behind the gas pump building, and the top left shows a glimpse of the building to its left which is at the same grade level as the gas pump building. The now photo below shows a newer building which is in about the same position as the old gas pump building. The lower grade buildings were behind it. That area has been filled in directly behind the building and the back grade has been raised. The original below grade buildings ran from just to the right of the now building to about half-way to the left to the trees. There, the regular grade building was located.

## Behind the Gas Pump Building

The lower grade buildings can be seen above as well as a glimpse of the regular grade building ("Magazine Writer"). This road behind these buildings is no longer as the lower grade building site and the road have been raised. In the now photo below, the buildings and road above would be beneath the raised grade on the right.

The episodes which used the Mountain Patrol Station 2 on Mulholland Drive for filming were:

"Armored Car"
"Copter Cave In"
"Detour to Death"
"Diversion Robbery"
"Double Copter"
"Hired Killer"
"Hostage-Copter"
"Hostage Family Copter"
"Hot Cargo"
"Hypo Bandit"
"Kidnap Copter"
"Magazine Writer"
"Mexican Chase"
"Migrant Workers"
"Motorcycle" (season 2)
"Nitro"
"Tear Gas Copter"
"Witness Wife"
"Woman Escapes"

Located in the city of Newhall, it was originally called San Fernando Road. With the renaming of the street, a renumbering also occurred.

A house at 24317 Newhall Avenue was used in "Girl Bandit" and seen in the background in "Escort". The First Presbyterian Church was just down the street from it. That church was destroyed in an earthquake and a newer one was erected at the site of the house.

**Beginning at Hollywood Boulevard, this road heads up Nichols Canyon and almost reaches Mulholland Drive.**

*Top:* Looking south at the electrical supply station ("Explosives")
*Middle:* Looking north from the electrical supply station ("Explosives")
*Bottom:* Looking south from 2025 Nichols Canyon Road ("Temptation")

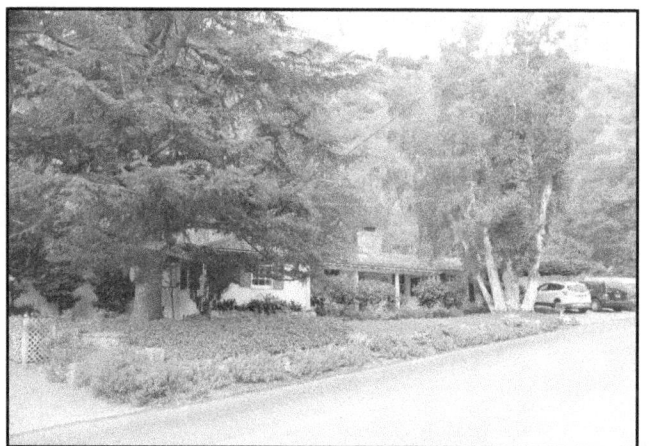

**2025 Nichols Canyon Road**

This house has had a remake in recent years. However, the two houses to its immediate north (right) have stayed the same. Seen in "Temptation".

Top: South of 2533 Nichols Canyon Road ("Explosives")
Middle: Intersection of Nichols Canyon Road and Del Zuro Drive ("Dead Patrolman")
Bottom: Intersetion of Nichols Canyon Road and La Cuesta Drive ("Dead Patrolman")

The intersection of Nichols Canyon Road and Willow Glen Road

**A short one block long street which connects with Culver Boulevard in Playa del Rey. Used in "Radioactive".**

*Top:* 1529 N. Ogden Drive
*Middle:* 1541 N. Ogden Drive
*Bottom:* 1542 N. Ogden Drive

*Top:* 1609 N. Ogden Drive
*Bottom:* 1623 N. Ogden Drive

# OLIVE STREET

**Starlite Motel was located at 3320 W. Olive Street in Burbank. Its entrance was on the corner of Lima Street. Used in "License Plates".**

**Located in Los Angeles, the alley between 11643 Otsego Street and Colfax Avenue was used in "Taxi" for a traveling shot.**

The bridge over Ballona Creek in Culver City was the location for the "Hit and Run" (season 1) accident scene.

Building, Street, House across the street

Bridge

Accident Site

MGM Backlot 3

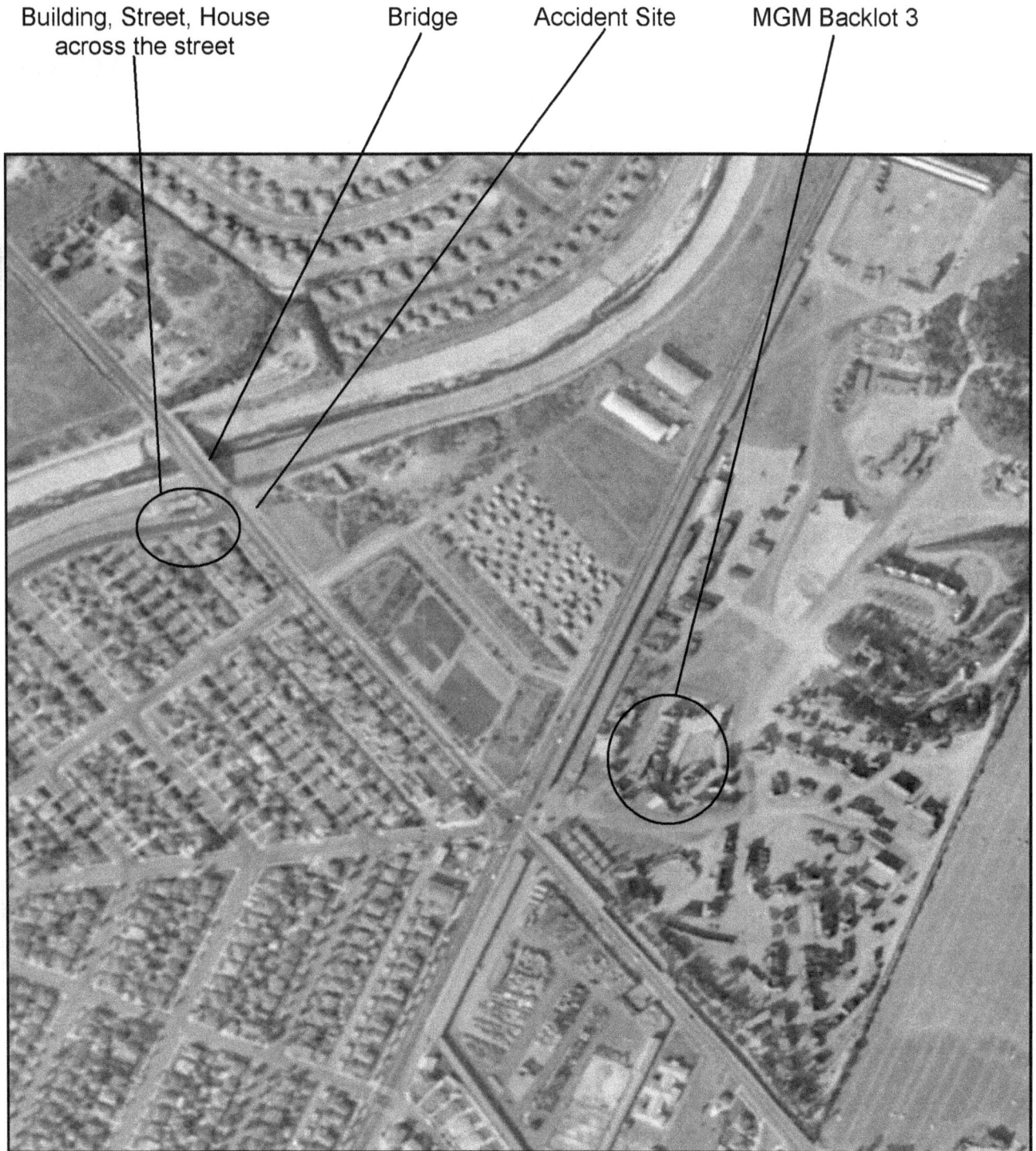

*Above:* A 1952 aerial showing the Overland Avenue bridge crossing of Ballona Creek

Across the street from the accident were, from left to right, a house (now an apartment building), a street (Ocean Drive), and an unidentified building (now gone).

*Top Left:* The bridge as seen in "Hit and Run" (season 1)
*Middle Left:* The bridge currently
*Top Right:* The steeple of the church which is seen in the top left image
*Bottom:* A Closeup of the bridge

The rear sides of a few movie sets on the Metro-Goldwyn-Mayer Lot 3 can be seen in the background; one to the left of the actors and another one between them. Below is the same view, but the backlot is gone and the view is blocked by buildings.

# OWENSMOUTH AVENUE

**Located in Chatsworth just south of Devonshire Street, the house at 10210 Owensmouth Avenue was used in "Safecracker".**

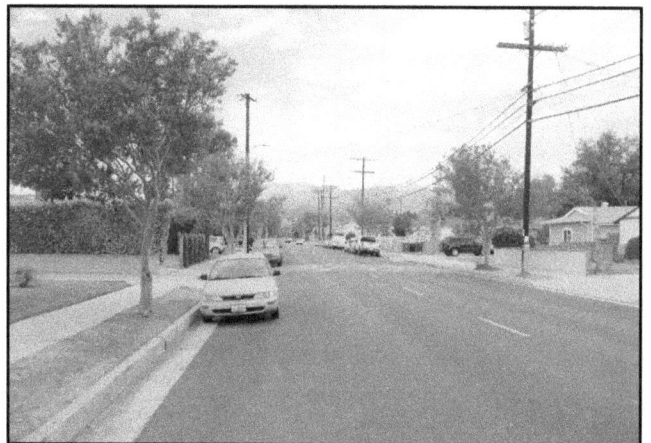

*Bottom:* Owensmouth Avenue looking north from 10210

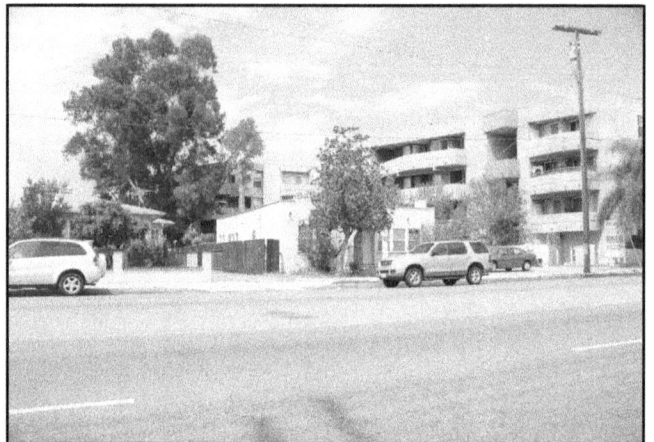

# PACIFIC COAST HIGHWAY

**Also known as Highway 1, a section of the road north of Malibu, at 28128 Pacific Coast Highway, along the beach at Paradise Cove and just south of it was used in "Harbor Story".**

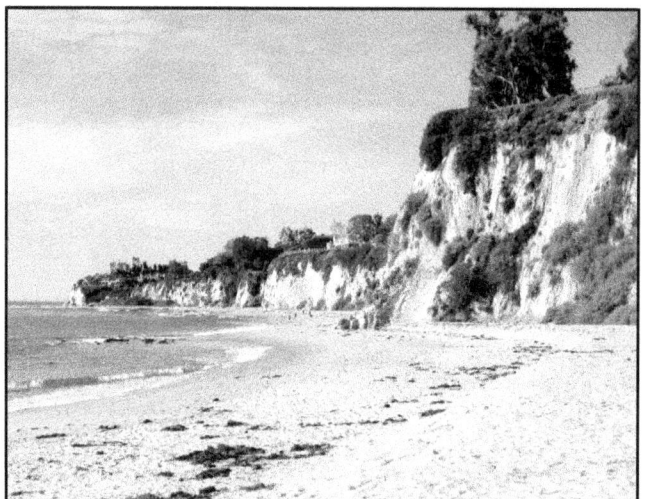

*Top:* The original pier was damaged in a storm in 1983 and is now much shorter in length
*Middle and Bottom:* Looking north from Paradise Cove

*Above:* Two views filmed south of Paradise Cove

Located in Marina del Rey, the farm used in "Hit and Run" (season 1) is now mostly under water.

The old Hughes Airport along W. Jefferson Boulevard is visible in the background of the middle left image. Loyola Marymount University is located in the hills in the lower left image.

Located in El Segundo, Library Park's fountain, now converted into a planter, and its arbor sitting area are in the northwest section of the park. It was used in "Lookout".

## PANAMA STREET
**Located in Los Angeles just east of Marina del Rey, this street was used in "Hit and Run" (season 1).**

*Top:* 12961 Panama Street
*Bottom:* Leaving 12961 Panama Street, heading east

**Located in the city of San Fernando, the Community Park has changed somewhat in appearance since filming of "Escort".**

The Community Park is located at 208 Park Avenue.
Above are views looking to the east at the park.

A row of houses across Park Avenue from the Community Park.
Some of the houses still remain.

# PLUMMER STREET

A ranch, located in Northridge just north of Plummer Street and bounded by Bothwell Road, Melvin Avenue, Citronia Street, and Ballinger Street, was used in "Fire".

The images on this page show four scenes from the show and one current view of the area. See next page for an aerial view of the ranch.

Above is a 1972 aerial view of the ranch. The street on the south side is Plummer Street, the one on the left side is Corbin Avenue, and the one at the top is Superior Street. Within a few years, this entire ranch was subdivided into housing.

# POINSETTIA DRIVE
**Located in West Hollywood, it is only one block in length. Used in "Convict's Wife".**

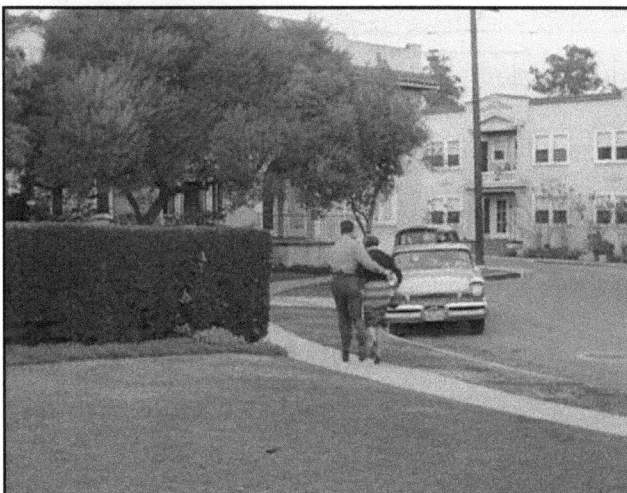

*Top:* 1233 Poinsettia Drive
*Middle:* Apartments, 1241 N. Poinsettia Place
*Bottom:* Apartments, 1256 N. Poinsettia Place

## POINSETTIA PLACE

This street was the east boundary of the ZIV Studio. A block south and a block north of the studio were used in "Armored Car", "Missing Witness", and "Typhoid Carrier".

*Top:* 1165 Poinsettia Place ("Armored Car")
*Middle:* Poinsettia Place north towards Hampton Avenue ("Armored Car")
*Bottom:* 936 Poinsettia Place acting as HP Headquarters ("Typhoid Carrier")

# RAILROAD AVENUE
This street parallels the Southern Pacific, now Metrolink, tracks in Saugus and Newhall. The Saugus Cafe at 25861 Railroad Avenue was used in "Girl Bandit".

*Top:* White building fronts on Central Avenue (see Central Avenue for a front view).
*Bottom:* This building, long gone, was next to the Southern Pacific train tracks just north of the Glendale depot; the water tower in the upper left was to the north of Los Feliz Boulevard.

300

# RANCH ROAD
## Located in Culver City adjacent to Eveward Road. Used in "Radioactive".

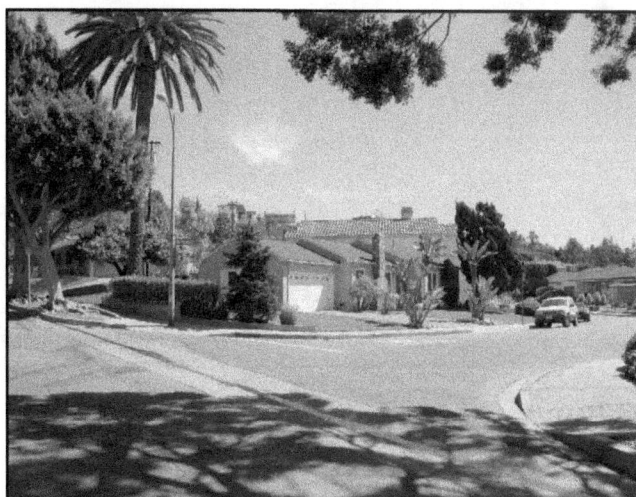

*Top and Middle:* Ranch Road looking eastward
*Bottom:* Turning onto Eveward Road

**Located in Northridge. Most of the episodes shot within a two-block vicinity of the Southern Pacific train depot.**

*Top:* Mick's Grill, 8322 Reseda Boulevard ("Narcotics Racket")
*Middle:* 8627 Reseda Boulevard ("Train Copter")
*Bottom:* Northridge Lumber Company, 8703 Reseda Boulevard ("Fire")

*Top:* Northridge Train Depot just east of Reseda Boulevard ("Fire"); depot long gone
*Middle:* Zelzah Warehouse, 8725 Reseda Boulevard, was located between the Northridge
Lumber Company and the train tracks ("Train Coper")
*Bottom:* Merritt Lumber Company, 8727 Reseda Boulevard , just north of the train tracks
("Train Copter")

*Top:* Allen's Northridge Market, 8738 Reseda Boulevard ("Fire")
*Middle:* 8805 Reseda Boulevard ("Confession")
*Bottom:* Paint Store, 8814 Reseda Boulevard ("Narcotics Racket")

*Top:* "Narcotics
Racket"
*Bottom:* "Confession"

8827 to 8833 Reseda Boulevard

*Top:* 8834 Reseda Boulevard ("Confession")
*Middle:* 8900 Reseda Boulevard ("Confession")
*Bottom:* 8900 block Reseda Boulevard as seen from Rayen Street ("Confession")

A major artery in the San Fernando Valley running east-west. Three locations were used in three episodes: "Hot Rod", "Motel Robbery", and "Typhoid Carrier".

*Top and Middle:* 20851 Roscoe Boulevard ("Hot Rod")
*Bottom:* Busch Brewery in background, near 16000 Roscoe Boulevard ("Motel Robbery")

A 1952 aerial showing the Curragh Stock Farm located at 22901 Roscoe Boulevard ("Typhoid Carrier"). Roscoe Boulevard is the street below center running left/right. The Farm is in the middle, just to the right of the lake.

The Curragh Stock Farm ("Typhoid Carrier"). Below is the approximate entrance to the ranch, now long gone.

**Located in the Los Feliz section of Los Angeles, south of Griffith Park. Used in "Framed Cop"**

*Top:* Rowena Avenue
*Middle:* 3476 Rowena Avenue
*Bottom:* 3464 Rowena Avenue

**In Woodland Hills, there is a pedestrian underpass to the 101 freeway which connects with Sale Avenue on both sides. Seen in the background of "The Trap".**

**This street was a major road prior to the freeways. Portions of it in the city of San Fernando, Sylmar, and Glendale were used.**

*Top and Middle:* 638 San Fernando Road at Ilex Street ("Escort")
*Bottom:* 1201 San Fernando Road ("Machine-Napping")

313

*Top:* Bank of America, 1148 San Fernando Road ("Machine-Napping)
*Middle:* The rear of 1148 San Fernando Road ("Machine-Napping)
*Bottom:* San Fernando Road under Interstate 5, looking south ("Escort")

314

*Top:* Mayfair Market, 1320 San Fernando Road ("Escort")
*Middle:* Bank of America, San Fernando Road and Cerritos Avenue
("Gem Robbery" season 4)
*Bottom:* Apartments to right of bank at San Fernando Road and Cerritos Avenue
("Express Delivery")

*Top:* Taylor Yard, now Rio de Los Angeles State Park ("Blood Money")
*Bottom:* A vintage shot, from the opposite direction, of the yard

Taylor's Milling Company, later owned by Ralston Purina, is the large white building in the top image, located on the SE corner of San Fernando Road and Elm Street.

*Facing Page:* A 1952 aerial of the Taylor Yard and two now photos

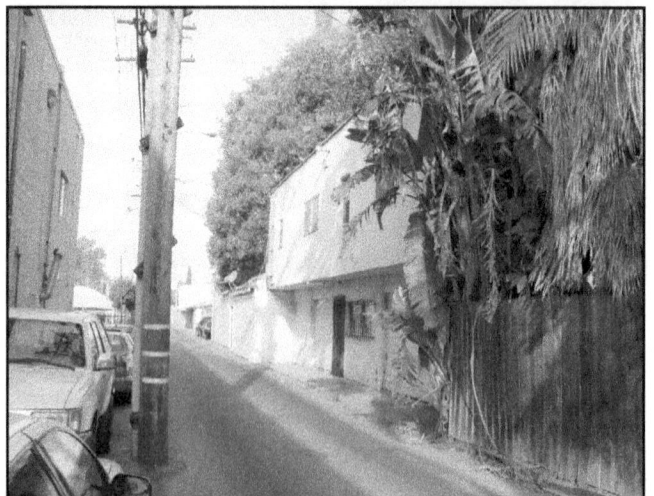

**Hal Jaffe Auto Repair**
7601 Santa Monica Boulevard
"Brave Boy"
*Bottom:* Alley behind 7601 Santa Monica Boulevard

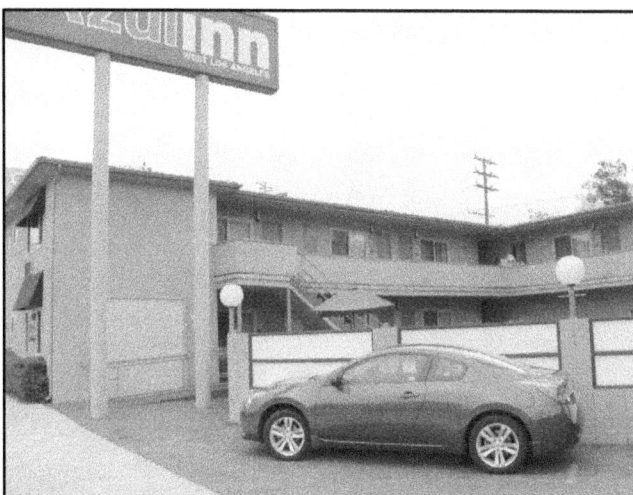

**Travelodge**
10740 Santa Monica Boulevard
"Stolen Car Ring"

*Top:* Paul's Radio Service, 8870 Santa Monica Boulevard ("Armored Car")
*Middle:* Thrifty Drugs, 8901 Santa Monica Boulevard ("Plant Robbery")
*Bottom:* Heading east from 8840 Santa Monica Boulevard ("Armored Car")

*Top:* Shermart, 8840 Santa Monica Boulevard ("Armored Car")
*Middle:* Hotel, 8869 Santa Monica Boulevard ("Armored Car")
*Bottom:* Commercial Casting Co, 8857 Santa Monica Boulevard ("Plant Robbery")

The West Hollywood Sheriff's Station is now located where Shermart used to be; on the SE corner of Santa Monica Boulevard and San Vicente Boulevard.

*Top:* Kay & Art's Cafe, 8785 Santa Monica Boulevard ("Plant Robbery")
*Bottom:* California Super Service (out of sight at right), 8797 Santa Monica Boulevard ("Plant Robbery")

1952 AERIAL

The Sherman Yard in West Hollywood was the property of Southern Pacific and was used by its Pacific Electric subsidiary. Interurban rail service ended in 1954 and only freight trains used the property after that.

The rectangle above is the location of the Shermart. The pentagon is the SP/PE Sherman Yard.

The northern portion of the property not owned by the Sheriff's Department, is part of the Metropolitan Transit District—buses now instead of trolleys and trains.

*Top Left:* "Temptation"
*All Others:* "Hit and Run" (season 3)

The Pacific Design Center (see now images at left) now sits on the lower portion of the old Sherman Yard.

*Top Left:* ("Hit and Run" season 3)

*Top Right:* ("Temptation")

The old Iverson Movie Ranch was located in the Santa Susana Mountains northwest of Chatsworth with an entrance road off of Santa Susana Pass Road. "Plane Crash" was the only episode in the series which used a movie ranch instead of real locations.

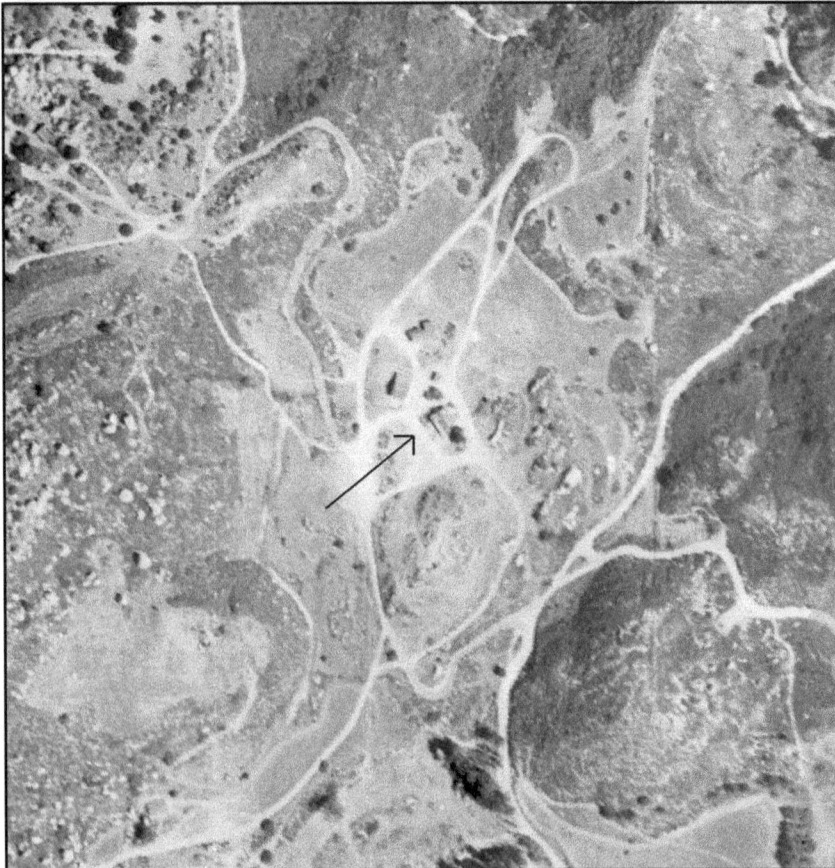

"Plane Crash" used the caretaker's house on the ranch. The house was built in such a way that all four sides could be used for filming, there being four entrances. The aerial at the left has an arrow pointed at the house. The now image above right is the exact location where the house used to stand. It was gone by 1969, possibly due to a wildfire.

The ranch house location is shown with the rectangle on the right side of the above recent aerial. The oval indicates the area for the scene below.

The right "now" photo was taken in 1985. The area has since been subdivided into 1 to 2 acre lots with mansion sized homes on the lots. The area is closed to the public except for a trail to gain access to the mountain to the north of the area. The left "then" image was taken at the bottom of the hill I was standing on to take the now photo and is to the right edge and off of it.

The airplane scenes were shot on the lower section of the ranch (the rest of the episode was shot on the upper and middle sections). In the above aerial, in the middle you can see a street with buildings. That was the western street set. To its left was the Wee Willie Winkle set. The trees around that area are not found elsewhere on the property and they can be seen in the image to the left. This area of the ranch has also changed greatly since the 1960's. Condominiums, a trailer park, and a major freeway now sit where thousands of movies and television shows had been filmed.

**Located on the west side of Los Angeles, two small areas of this street were used in "Stolen Car Ring".**

*Top:* Lakewood National Bank, 11944 San Vicente Boulevard
*Middle:* Alleyway between 11969 and 11975 San Vicente Boulevard, across from bank
*Bottom:* Knitting Circle, 11975 San Vicente Boulevard, across from bank

The intersection of San Vicente Boulevard and La Mesa Drive. The house, second from the corner, in the upper left image, is still there but hard to see from street level due to foliage growth.

*Top:* Greene's Jewelers, 17322 Saticoy Street ("Safecracker")
*Middle:* Greene's Jewelers, 17322 Saticoy Street ("Trailer Story")
*Bottom:* Looking out the doorway of Greene's Jewelers ("Trailer Story")

*Top:* The rear of Greene's Jewelers, 17322 Saticoy Street ('Safecracker")
*Bottom:* Departing from the rear of Greene's Jewelers,
heading east in the alley ("Safecracker")

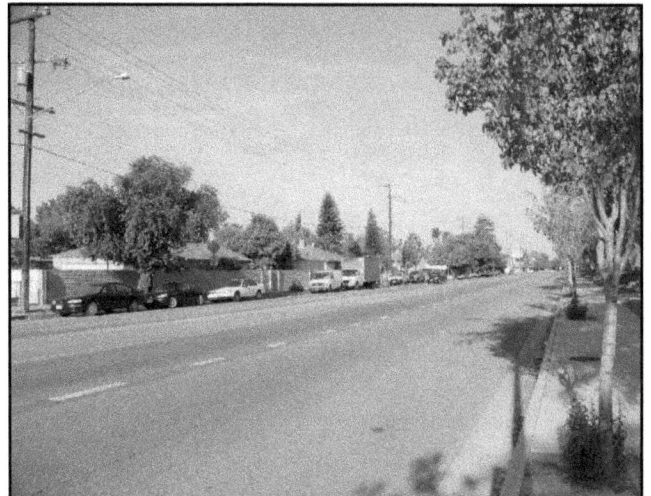

**Traveling Shot**
Along Saticoy Street, pass Gaynor Avenue,
and right turn into an empty field east of Van Nuys Airport
"Motel Robbery"

**Traveling Shot**
Vacant lot on north side of Saticoy Street near Gaynor Avenue
Van Nuys Airport hangers can be seen in middle left image
"Motel Robbery"

Located in Burbank, an area around an alley north of Clark Avenue and west of N. Hollywood Way was used in "License Plates".

*Top:* 814 N. Screenland Drive, next to alley
*Middle:* 815 N. Screenland Drive
*Bottom:* 819 N. Screenlad Drive

## SELMA AVENUE

**Located west of Hollywood and south of Hollywood Boulevard, a short stretch of this street was used in "Brave Boy".**

*Top:* House behind Boyett is located at 1556 Courtney Avenue, just south of Selma Avenue
*Middle:* Intersection of Selma Avenue and Courtney Avenue
*Bottom:* Heading east on Selma Avenue from Ogden Drive

336

# SEMRAD ROAD

**In West Hills, there used to be a large ranch near the intersection of Valley Circle Boulevard and Vanowen Street. The ranch barn used in "Stripped Cars" was located approximately south of Semrad Road and Bell Creek.**

El Escorpion Peak can be seen in the top images. It is a very prominent feature of the area. The ranch was still in full swing in 1952, but by 1959, a lot of it had been subdivided.

**A section of this street in the San Fernando Valley was used in two episodes: "Lie Detector" and "Motel Robbery".**

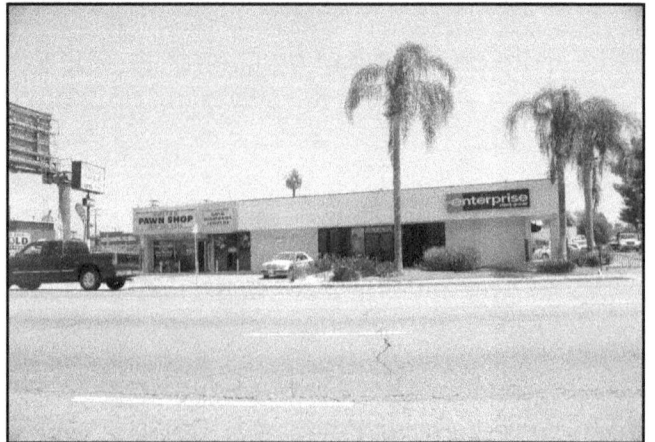

*Top:* Real Estate, 7246 Sepulveda Boulevard ("Lie Detector")
*Middle:* Deeks Realty, 7500 Sepulveda Boulevard ("Lie Detector")
*Bottom:* Rita Curtis Swim School, 8220 Sepulveda Boulevard ("Motel Robbery")

**San Fernando Valley Motel**
7533 Sepulveda Boulevard
"Lie Detector"

**Monticello Hotel**
8071 Sepulveda Boulevard
"Motel Robbery"

**Panorama Motel**
8209 Sepulveda Boulevard
"Motel Robbery"

The Pacific Lodge Youth Services is located at 4900 Serrania Avenue in Woodland Hills and was used in "Gambling".

**This street was used in "The Search" and "Statute of Limitations" and can be seen in the background of scenes in "Phony Insurance".**

*Top and Middle:* The rear of 18238 Sherman Way portrayed HP Headquarters ("Statute of Limitations")
*Bottom:* Anitas, 18361 Sherman Way ("Phony Insurance")

343

*Top:* McMahan Furniture Store, 18344 Sherman Way ("Statute of Limitations")
*Middle and Bottom:* Probably North Hollywood Concrete Tile Company, 12323 Sherman Way ("The Search")

**The Joe Hran Texaco Station and the Log Cabin Motel next door were located on the SE corner of Sierra Highway and Soledad Canyon Road in Santa Clarita.**

The Joe Hran Texaco Station was seen in "Girl Bandit" and "Reformed Criminal". The Log Cabin Motel is seen in "Girl Bandit".

## SOLEDAD CANYON ROAD

**Located in Saugus, for many years it ran pass the Hoot Gibson Rodeo Arena, later Bonelli Arena, then the Saugus Speedway, now a Swap Meet.**

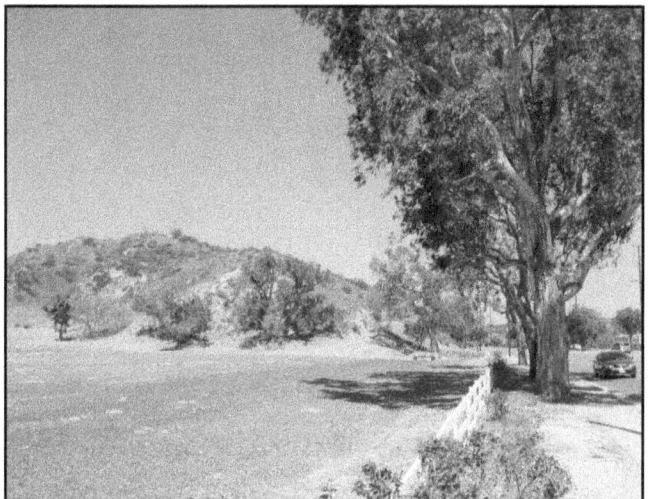

Scenes from "Gil Bandit"

**Located in West Hollywood. The locations used in "Killer on the Run" and "Gambling Story" were located just north and just south of Melrose Avenue.**

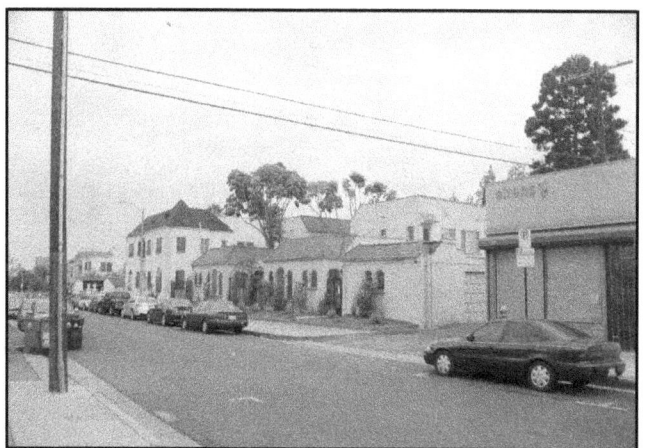

*Top:* Young Israel, 660 N. Spaulding Avenue ("Killer on the Run"

*Middle:* Stone Printing Co., 681 N. Spaulding Avenue ("Killer on the Run")

*Bottom:* Apartments, 631-649 N. Spaulding Avenue ("Killer on the Run")

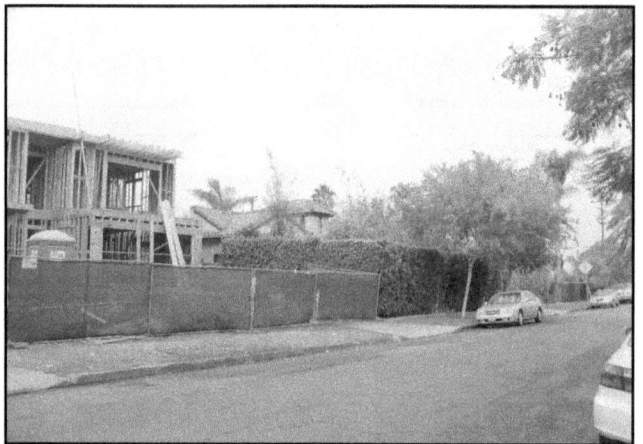

*Top:* 740 N. Spaulding Avenue ("Gambling Story")
*Middle:* 734 N. Spaulding Avenue ("Gambling Story")
*Bottom:* 728 N. Spaulding Avenue ("Gambling Story")

## STADIUM WAY

**Stadium Way was originally named Chavez Ravine Road. The Old Lodge, now known as Montecillo de Leo Politi, is located in Elysian Park with an entrance road just north of Scott Avenue. Used in "Foster Child". The old Barlow Sanitarium is just south of Scott Avenue. Used in "Family Affair".**

Left three images from "Foster Child"
and show the area around the entrance to the Old Lodge

Two left images from "Foster Child" and show a historic 1950's view of the Old Lodge area. Right two images are generic shots of that same general area as it appears today.

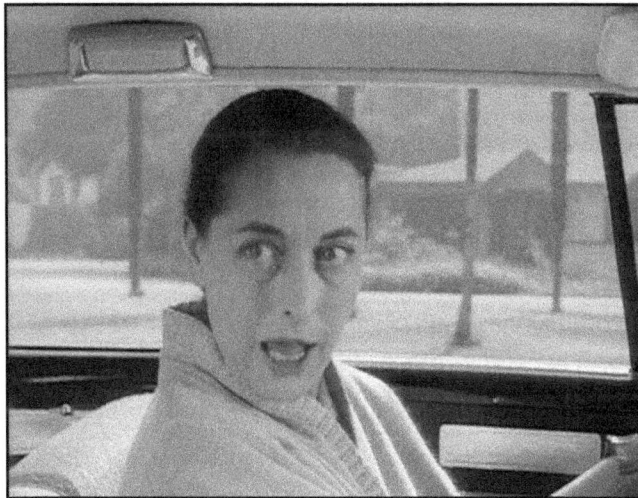

The old Barlow Sanitarium is now the Barlow Respiratory Hospital
"Family Affair"

The old Barlow Sanitarium is now the Barlow Respiratory Hospital
"Family Affair"

*Top:* 4101 Stansbury Avenue
*Middle:* Intersection of Stansbury Avenue and Roblar Road
*Bottom:* Looking a little farther up Roblar Road from Stansbury Avenue

The location of this ranch house is on empty land just north of the parking lot north of Beverly Park Street in the hills of Beverly Hills. It was used in three episodes: "Ranch-Copter", "Tear Gas Copter", and "Witness Wife".

**Hill-Top Ranch House**
The house is the white topped building inside the oval.
The entrance to the property was from the north.
You can see another house to the left and up from the hill-top house.

*Top:* Then entrance road on the north side of the property; now entrance road is on the south side of a gated community ("Witness Wife")
*Middle:* The house close to the hill-top house ("Ranch-Copter")
*Bottom:* An aerial view of the house ("Tear Gas Copter")

*Top:* Front view of house which faced south ("Tear Gas Copter")
*Middle:* An open shelter building through which you entered the ranch house parking ("Witness Wife")
*Bottom:* An outbuilding("Witness Wife")

**Located in Los Angeles County, it begins at Olvera Street in Downtown Los Angeles and heads to the Pacific Ocean, ending in Santa Monica. Along the way, a portion is the old Route 66, and another area is the famed Sunset Strip.**

*Top:* The "False Confession" man is standing in a corner of the gas station which used to stand at 1106 Sunset Boulevard

*Bottom:* Across the street from the above gas station was the Paradise Motel at 1116 Sunset Boulevard along Route 66 ("False Confession")

*Top:* Harrington Motel, 5224 Sunset Boulevard ("Rabies")
*Middle:* TraveLodge, 7370 Sunset Boulevard ("Killer on the Run")
*Bottom:* Brentwood Motor Hotel, 12200 W. Sunset Boulevard ("Christmas Story")

*Top:* 7801 Sunset Boulevard ("Temptation")
*Bottom:* 7758 Sunset Boulevard ("Brave Boy")

Located in Sherman Oaks and used in "Diversion Robbery". The apartments are still there as well as the grocery store.

*Top and Middle:* Grocery Store, 4529 Sylmar Avenue
*Bottom:* Sylmar Palms Apartments, 4555 Sylmar Avenue

This is a major north-south route on the west side of the San Fernando Valley. It is designated Route 27.

*Top and Middle:* The Wooden Shoe, 8240 Topanga Canyon Boulevard ("Typhoid Carrier")
*Bottom:* Chatsworth Lumber, 9754 Topanga Canyon Boulevard ("Motorcycle" season 1)

*Top:* Chatsworth Community Church, 10051 Topanga Canyon Boulevard ("Safecracker")
The church was moved to the Oakwood Cemetery .
*Middle and Bottom:* Gas Station, 10124 Topanga Canyon Boulevard ("Ex-Con")
The house was adjacent, on the south side, to the gas station.

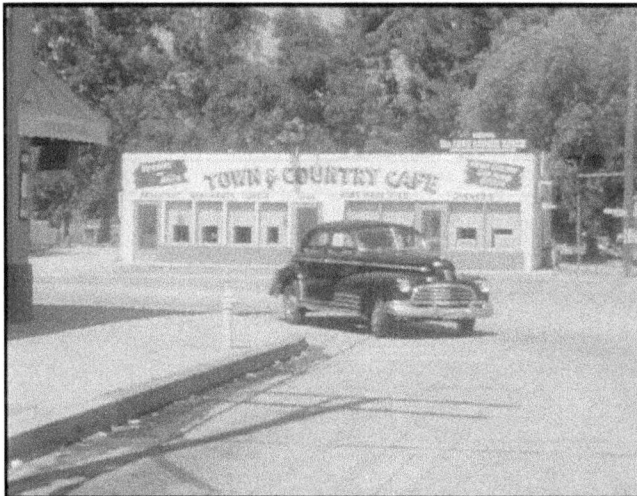

You will notice a sign on the right side roof of Town & Country Cafe. One says "Corriganville", the other "The Lone Ranger Ranch". They are referring to the same movie ranch: Corriganville. For just over two years it was "The Lone Ranger Ranch".

*Top:* Chatsworth Market, 10249 Topanga Canyon Boulevard ("Motorcycle" season 1)
*Middle:* Town & Country Cafe, 10255 Topanga Canyon Boulevard ("Motorcycle" season 1)
*Bottom:* Town & Country Cafe ("Safecracker")

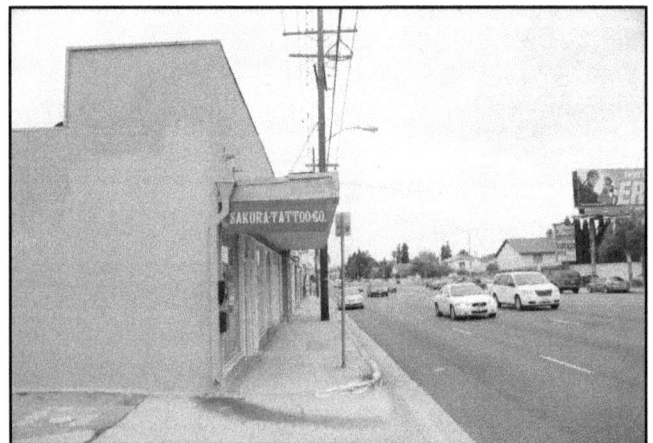

*Top:* Topanga Canyon Boulevard and Andora Avenue ("Fake Cop")
*Middle:* Topanga Canyon Boulevard and Marilla Street ("Motorcycle" season 1)
*Bottom:* 10242 Topanga Canyon Boulevard ("Safecracker")

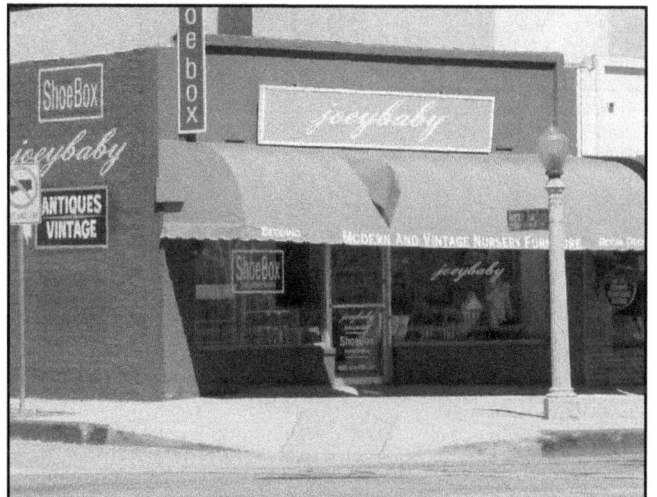

*Top:* Topanga Canyon Boulevard looking north towards Parthenia Street ("Hitchhiker")
*Middle:* Topanga Canyon Boulevard looking south towards Plummer Street ("Hitchhiker")
*Bottom:* 5305 Topanga Canyon Boulevard ("Anti-Toxin")

**This street is one block north of and parallel to Chatsworth Street. It was used in "Female Hitchhiker".**

*Top:* Car is heading west on Tulsa Street from Topanga Canyon Boulevard
*Bottom:* Car is turning from Tulsa Street onto Farralone Avenue

# VALLEY CIRCLE BOULEVARD
**Located in Chatsworth, a section on the north side of the Chatsworth Reservoir was used in "Ex-Con" and "Mental Patient".**

*Top:* Once a private driveway, it is now a continuation of Plummer Street ("Ex-Con")
*Middle and Bottom:* Views of both directions along Chatsworth Reservoir just west of Plummer Street ("Mental Patient")

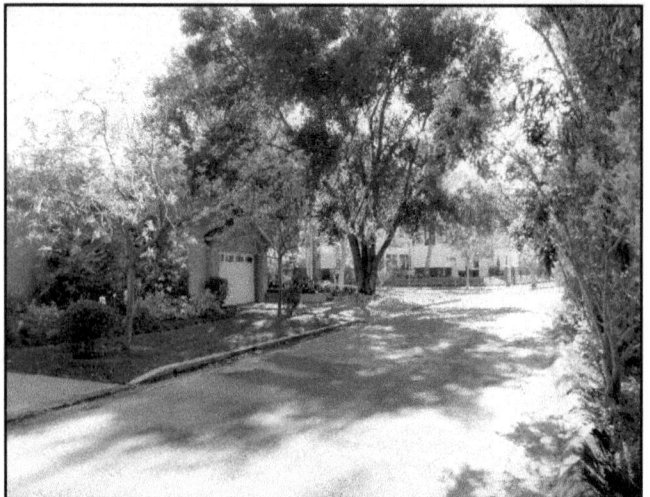

*Top:* Heading west on Valleyheart Drive passing Valley Spring Lane
*Middle:* Passing Goodland  Avenue
*Bottom:* The side of a house facing Valleyheart Drive (address is 4205 Goodland Avenue)

*Top:* The west and south corner of the house facing Valleyheart Drive
(house front is at 4205 Goodland Avenue
*Bottom:* Turning north on Alcove Avenue from Valleyheart Drive

*Top:* Corner of Valley Spring Lane and Bellaire Avenue
*Middle and Bottom:* Weddington Golf Course in background

*Top:* Intersection of Vanalden Avenue and Kinzie Street ("Confession")
*Middle and Bottom:* 9839 Vanalden Avenue ("Confession")

*Top:* Looking south on Vanalden Avenue from across the street from 9857 Vanalden Avenue ("Dan Sick")
*Middle:* 9857 Vanalden Avenue ("Hot Rod")
*Bottom:* 9857 Vanalden Avenue ("Dan Sick")

Two blocks west of Vanalden Avenue along Kinzie Street is Beckford Avenue where the above scenes from "Narcotics Racket" were shot.

**Located in the city of Van Nuys in the San Fernando Valley, this airport was used in "Trailer Story".**

**The Norman Larson Company**
7240 Hayvenhurst Place

Based on aerial photographs of the area, this company's building
was located approximately where the above now photo was taken.

**A major north-south street in the San Fernando Valley. Portions in Sherman Oaks and Van Nuys were used for filming.**

*Above:* Views of the Nahas Department Store at 4520 Van Nuys Boulevard ("Diversion Robbery")

The rear of this location can be seen in the Sylmar Avenue section.

*Top:* Sherman Oaks Vacuums, 4529 Van Nuys Boulevard ("Woman Escapes")
*Middle:* Erma May Robbins Cosmetics, 4531 Van Nuys Boulevard ("Woman Escapes")
*Bottom:* Joe Ole's Hardware, 4543 Van Nuys Boulevard ("Woman Escapes")

*Top:* 4645 Van Nuys Boulevard ("Expose")
*Middle and Bottom:* 5539 Van Nuys Boulevard ("Expose")

*Above:* Sportmans Lodge, 12825 Ventura Boulevard ("Split Robbery")

The Sportsman Lodge can be seen in the background where the bad guy drives into the Hughes Market parking lot at 12842 Ventura Boulevard.

**Hughes Market, now Ralphs**
12842 Ventura Boulevard
"Split Robbery"

*Above Images:* Alley behind 13629 Ventura Boulevard ("Human Bomb")

380

*Top:* Tropi Kool Pools, 13865 Ventura Boulevard ("Double Cross")
*Middle:* Escrow Guarantee, 13900 Ventura Boulevard ("Double Cross")
*Bottom:* Behind Escrow Guarantee, 13900 Ventura Boulevard ("Double Cross")

**Maple Leaf Motel**
13901 Ventura Boulevard
*Top Left:* "Expose"   *Top Right:* "Double Cross"

*Top:* Rand's Ventura Round-Up, 13920 Ventura Boulevard ("Mistaken Identity")
*Middle:* Steele's Motor Lodge, 13949 Ventura Boulevard ("Split Robbery")
*Bottom:* Ralphs, 14049 Ventura Boulevard ("Split Robbery")

*Top and Middle*: Ventura Boulevard and Hazeltine Avenue ("Split Robbery")
*Bottom:* Sherman Oaks Jewelers, 14522 Ventura Boulevard ("Diversion Robbery")

*Top and Middle:* Victory Motel, 15052 Ventura Boulevard ("Deadly Diamonds")
*Bottom:* Huckins Steaks, 17301 Ventura Boulevard ("Narcotics Racket")

385

*Top and Middle:* Encino TraveLodge 16117 Ventura Boulevard ("Resort")
*Bottom:* A & B Motors, 19326 Ventura Boulevard ("Hitchhiker")

*Top:* Encino Oaks Motor Lodge, 17323 Ventura Boulevard ("Narcotics Racket")
*Middle:* Neider's Body Shop, 22440 Ventura Boulevard ("The Trap")
*Bottom:* Woodland Hills Pet Shop, 22543 Ventura Boulevard ("The Trap")

*Top:* Lee's Steak House Hideaway Room, 22611 Ventura Boulevard ("The Trap")
*Middle:* Merrill's Feed & Saddlery, 22705 Ventura Boulevard ("The Trap")
*Bottom:* William R. Wilson Jr. Insurance, 22708 Ventura Boulevard ("The Trap")

*Top:* Wising Well Cafe, 22941 Ventura Boulevard ("Released Convict")
*Middle:* Ventura Boulevard and Alhama Drive ("Gambling")
*Bottom:* Ventura Boulevard west of 101 freeway exit ("The Trap")

# 1959 Aerial
## Golden Pheasant Restaurant/Billingsley Steak Ranch
## and Motel in Calabasas

Motel

Golden Pheasant/Billingsley

Ventura Boulevard/101 Freeway

When the pilot episode was filmed, this property at 26300 Ventura Boulevard was known as the Golden Pheasant Restaurant ("Road Block"). In early 1957, it became Billingsley's Steak Ranch as new owners took over. Ventura Boulevard in this area became highway 101, and later it was turned into a freeway.

Next door to the Golden Pheasant Restaurant/Billingsley Steak Ranch was a motel ("Frightened Witness").

Walking south on Ventura Canyon Avenue towards Ventura Boulevard. Passing 4321 Ventura Canyon Avenue before turning west into the alley (see Ventura Boulevard).

The three images at left are different views of Eugene's Credit Jewelers. Above is a current view of the location.

**Eugenes Credit Jewelers**
1745 N. Vermont Avenue
"Hypo Bandit"

**2535 N. Vermont Avenue**
"Suspected Cop"

**VERMONT CANYON**

Vermont Avenue heads up into Vermont Canyon of Griffith Park.The entrance to the park is seen in the top images ("Hypo Bandit"). The thin tree has grown over the past 50 years. Near the Greek Theater is the curve in the road where the above scene was filmed ("Suspected Cop").

## VERMONT CANYON ROAD
**Vermont Avenue turns into Vermont Canyon Road once it enters Griffith Park. Near the Observatory is a tunnel used in "Machine-Napping".**

*Top:* The east tunnel entrance
*Bottom:* The west tunnel entrance

## VICTORY BOULEVARD

**Located in Valley Glen, this is a major east-west street in the San Fernando Valley. Used in "Slain Cabby" and "Trailer Story".**

*Top:* Knoll Crest Realty, 12800 Victory Boulevard ("Trailer Story")
*Middle:* Heading west to 12764 Victory Boulevard ("Trailer Story")
*Bottom:* 12764 Victory Boulevard ("Slain Cabby")

*Top:* "Double Death"
*Middle:* "Convicted Innocent"
*Bottom:* Looking northward on the opposite side of the street ("Convicted Innocent")
The now middle and bottom images show the opposite side of the street.

**Located in Marina del Rey. A ranch located near 608 Washington Boulevard was used in "Car Theft".**

Filmed at the intersection of Weddington Street
and Bakman Avenue

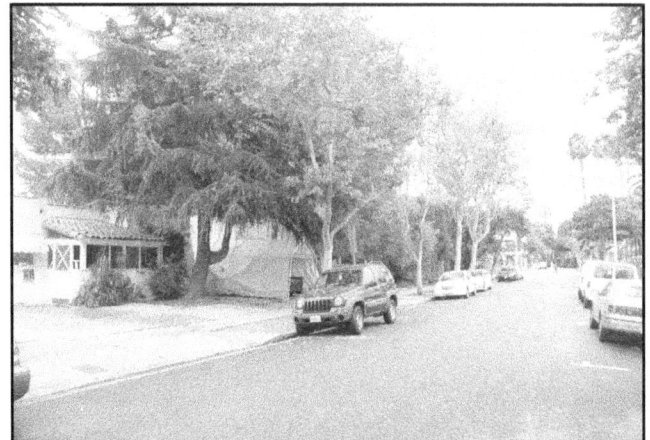

*Top:* 628 Westbourne Drive
*Middle:* 622 Westbourne Drive
*Bottom:* Westbourne Drive towards Melrose Avenue

**Furs by Lehrer**
1167 N. Western Avenue

## 1953 Aerial Northeast Corner of Whiteman Airport

Building 2    Building 1    Adjacent Ranch    Ranch Buildings

*Top:* Building 1 ("Efficiency Secretary")
*Middle:* Building 2 ("Stolen Plane-Copter"
*Bottom:* Adjacent Ranch ("Efficiency Secretary")

The location of the adjacent ranch is in the Shelter Isle Mobile Estates.

*Top:* North end of airstrip ("Stolen Plane-Copter")
*Middle:* The ranch buildings ("Efficiency Secretary")
*Bottom:* Four chimneys, near San Fernando Road and Sheldon Street ("Efficiency Secretary")

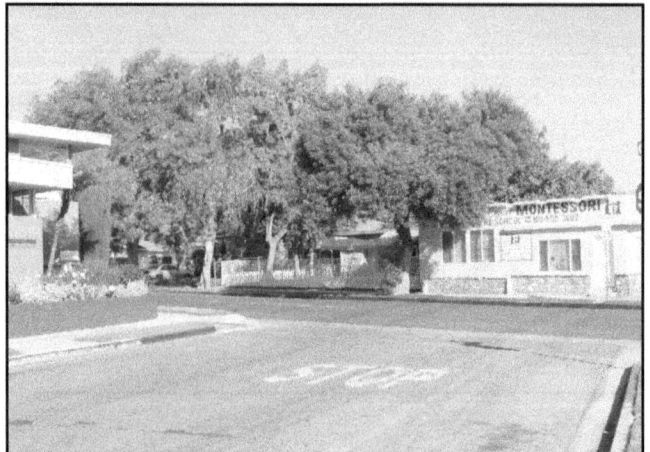

*Top and Middle:* Views of the church
*Bottom:* Intersection of Whitnall Highway and Clark Avenue

# WILCOX AVENUE

Located in Hollywood. A police station, fire station, and hospital are all found adjacent to one another. Featured in "License Plates".

Below is a historical look at the police station (on left) and hospital (on right). The fire station was behind and facing onto Cole Avenue.

## WILLOUGHBY AVENUE

Located in West Hollywood. A block near the ZIV Studio was used in "Runaway Boy". Just west of Highland Avenue there is an alley which runs north-south, from the old Bekins building southward. This alley was used in "Counterfeit" and "Girl Bandit".

*Top:* 7416 Willoughby Avenue ("Runaway Boy")
*Bottom:* Looking west along Willoughby Avenue from 7416 ("Runaway Boy")

*Top:* Apartments, 6851 Willoughby Avenue ("Counterfeit")
*Middle:* Apartments, 6815 Willoughby Avenue ("Counterfeit")
*Bottom:* Alley between Romaine Street and Willoughby Avenue ("Counterfeit")

*Top:* Exiting south from the alley a Willoughby Avenue ("Girl Bandit")
*Middle:* The rear of 901 N. Highland Avenue ("Girl Bandit")
NOTE: The door and windows have been bricked up
*Bottom:* The south side of the building at 901 N. Highland Avenue ("Counterfeit")

*Top:* The rear of 829 N. Highland Avenue ("Counterfeit")
*Middle:* Alley behind 831 N. Highland Avenue, looking south ("Counterfeit")
*Bottom:* Alley behind 831 N. Highland Avenue, looking north ("Counterfeit")

*Top:* North entrance to alley from Willoughby Avenue ("Counterfeit")
*Middle:* Crossing Willoughby Avenue from south to north at the alley ("Counterfeit")
*Bottom:* Backyards of 810-824 Citrus Avenue from the alley ("Counterfeit")

## WILLOW GLEN ROAD
Located in the Hollywood Hills between Laurel Canyon Boulevard and Nichols Canyon Road. The intersection with Woodstock Road was used in "Killer on the Run".

Located in Los Angeles. Frank's Nurseries at 12424 Wilshire Boulevard can be seen in "Stolen Car Ring".

**Located in Winnetka. Chuck's Fountain & Grill at 8257 Winnetka Avenue was used in "Hot Rod".**

In the background on the right in the bottom image you can see Bill's Market. It was located at 20059 Roscoe Boulevard.

**Located in Canoga Park. The intersection of Woodlake Avenue and Justice Street was used in "Scared Cop".**

*Bottom:* A short distance east of Woodlake Avenue and slightly north of the present Strathern Street was the above road next to a ranch—a current view of the area

**Located in Sherman Oaks, the Nifty Food Market at 4742 Woodman Avenue was used in "Slain Cabby".**

**Located in Woodland Hills. From Dumetz Road south a block, this street was used in "Released Convict".**

*Top and Middle:* Ybarra Road looking south; Dumetz Road is at the bottom of the top image
*Bottom:* Intersection of Ybarra Road and Dumetz Road (looking west on Dumetz Road)

# VENTURA COUNTY

## CONEJO VALLEY AIRPORT AREA

Located in Thousand Oaks, the second airport was situated south of the current 101 freeway. The area was used in "Retired Gangster".

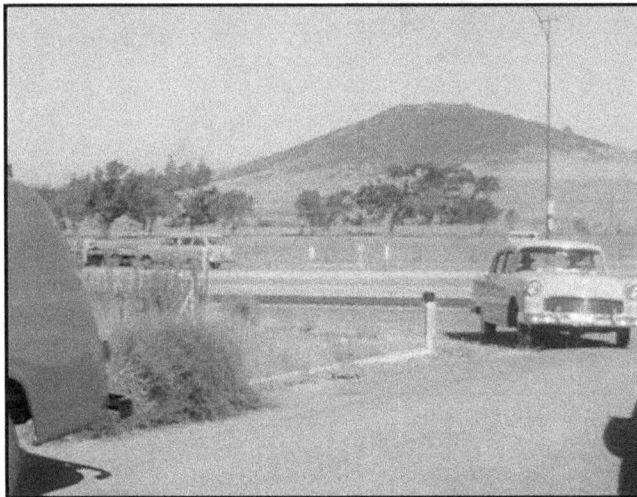

The current Moorpark Road on the south side of the 101 freeway runs where the old entrance road used to be.

*Top:* Highway 101 from the airport entrance road
*Middle:* Turning from Highway 101 onto the airport entrance road
*Bottom:* The airport entrance road as it curves westward

The black oval in the above aerial shot shows the east entrance to the second Conejo Airport. The remains of the first airport is just below the oval. The main road running east-west through the oval is Highway 101, now upgraded to the 101 freeway. The white rectangle shows the alignment of the runway of the airport. The filming for "Retired Gangster" was done in the oval. The current Moorpark Road runs through that area and all of the surrounding area has been subdivided into housing and a golf course.

## CRESCENT WAY

Located in Thousand Oaks and south of Thousand Oaks Boulevard. A house at 2884 Crescent Way was used in "Father Thief".

**GREENMEADOW DRIVE**
Located in Thousand Oaks at 288 Greenmeadow Drive, the Cameron Center was once a home of the Janss family (lower right of bottom image). Used in "Retired Gangster".

## LOS ANGELES AVENUE

Located in Simi Valley. The street runs east-west the breadth of the valley. The Southern Pacific Train Depot in Simi Valley was used in "Train Robbery". The depot has been saved and moved to Santa Susana.

*Top Left:* Original depot as filmed
*Top Right, Middle Left:* Depot now
*Middle Right:* Original location at 4465 Los Angeles Avenue
*Bottom:* Towing Garage, 4456 Los Angeles Avenue

427

This ranch is located north and west of Marin Street in the foothills above Thousand Oaks just west of Moorpark Road.

**Junior Department Store**
aka Nixon's 5 & 10 Dept. Store
3021 E. Thousand Oaks Boulevard

*Top:* As filmed
*Bottom Left:* Historical look
*Bottom Right:* Current view

*Top:* Conejo Pharmacy, 3041 E. Thousand Oaks Boulevard
*Bottom:* Max & Rose Cafe, 3006 E. Thousand Oaks Boulevard

Behind 2860 E. Thousand Oaks Boulevard
Used as Highway Patrol Headquarters
Original building has been replaced

# UNIDENTIFIED
# LOCATIONS

Out of the approximately 600 locations used in *Highway Patrol*, there were a few which I could not locate, and there were some which I did not look for (many of the traveling shots along Mulholland Drive). On this and the following pages are the locations I did not find during my research.

"Reckless Driving"
Most of this episode was filmed in El Segundo and a couple of areas around Los Angeles International Airport.

"Radioactive"
Playa del Rey and Culver City were used in this episode, but the above intersection of a Boulevard with a Drive I could not locate.

**"Mountain Copter"**
This shot of the entrance to a building numbered 180 was used as a stock shot in several episodes. I could not find this building.

**"Blast Area-Copter"**
These cabins appeared in this episode which was filmed in and around Bronson Canyon. Could these buildings have been part of the Hollywoodland Girl's Camp?

**"The Search" and "Hired Killer"**
This small market appeared in these two episodes. It may have been located in the Chatsworth area.

"Stolen Car Ring"
Most of this episode was filmed in the West Los Angeles area.

"Statute of Limitations"
Similar in appearance to the Shadow Ranch house, this ranch house is either gone or hiding from me.

"Migrant Workers"
Majority of this episode shot in the Santa Monica Mountains near Mulholland Drive in Encino.

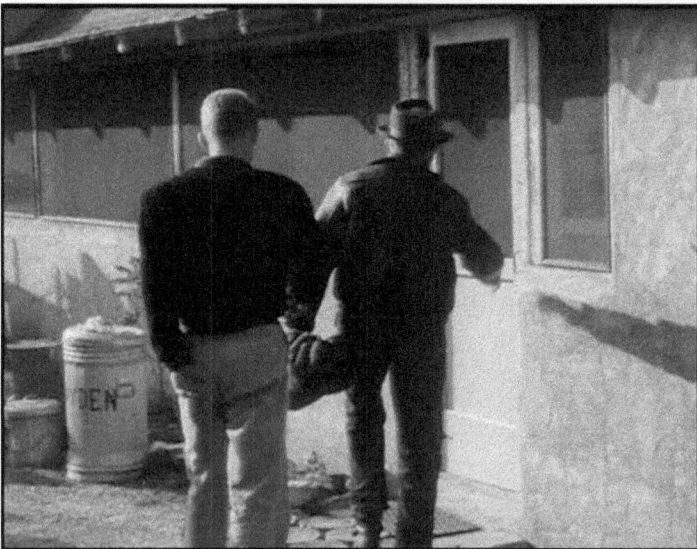

"Officer's Wife"
This building appeared as Highway Patrol headquarters in this episode.

"Office's Wife"
The above episode shot mostly around Canyon Drive, but I could not locate this house.

"Gem Robbery"
Located somewhere in the Los Feliz or Hollywood area, this gas station appears to be down and across from a large wooden structure which might have been a liquor store.

"Hostage-Copter"
The House of O'Shea had a street number of 12040. This diner was not in any telephone directories of the time period, nor any advertisements or articles in local newspapers.

439

Top: "Portrait of Death" This Drive Inn Hotel does not appear in any telephone directories of the time period nor in any advertisements or articles in local newspaprs. Its street number was 10400. Could it have been located on the southwest corner of Santa Monica Boulevard and Beverly Glen Boulevard, now an empty lot?

Bottom: "The Sniper" Street number appears to be "623". Most of the episode filmed at the Upper Franklin Canyon Reservoir area. Was this business somewhere in the vicinity of the ZIV Studio?

"Policewoman"

All three of these images appear to have been shot in the downtown Los Angeles vicinity. The top image and the middle image are across the street from each other. Wording on the building in the middle image says "Mfgr of Medicinal Products". The bottom image was probably somewhere nearby. One sign on a building seems to be starting the word "Coast". Consulting telephone directories and local newspapers, nothing "popped" up to identify this location.

"Blood Money"
All three images on this page are from this episode. Some of the scenes for this show were filmed at the old Southern Pacific Taylor Yard, which is now a park.

"Deadly Diamonds"
(Season 4)
This episode shot mainly around the Glendale area.

"Blood Money"
See facing page. Was this house in the vicinity of the apartment building?

"Auto Press"
The top image was across the street from the lower image. The gas station was a Mobilegas. A building across the street was a Los Angeles County Library. Part of the episode was shot in Carson.

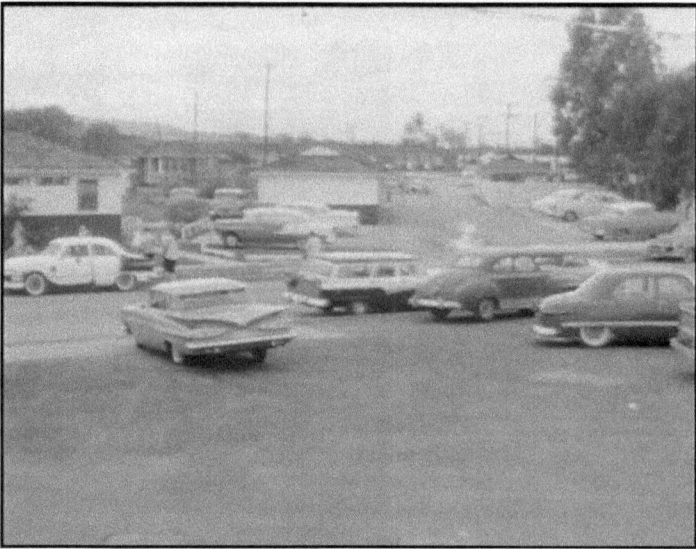

"Runaway Boy"
This building was probably on or near Martel Avenue in West Hollywood in close proximity to the ZIV Studio. The building is no longer there or it has been greatly altered in appearance. None of the buildings in that area have the three drain pipes in a row.

"Stolen Car Ring"
This motel was probably the Pacific Tourist Court at 2475 Lincoln Boulevard in Venice.

"Statute of Limitations"
These three images show the same intersection, located somewhere in the San Fernando Valley. Reseda was used for some scenes in the show.

"Statute of Limitations"
These three images are all at the same location somewhere in the San Fernando Valley. Reseda was used for some scenes in the show.

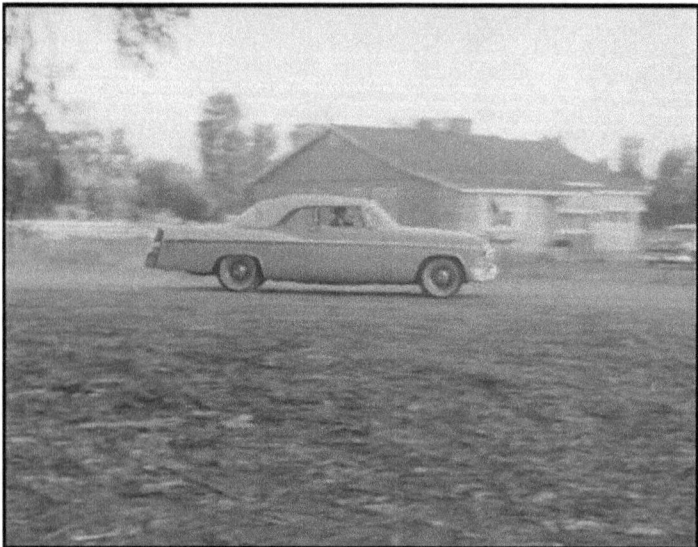

"Female Hitchhiker"
These three images show a traveling shot along a road. This is probably Chatsworth and the road may be Andora Avenue.

"Hired Killer"
These three images show different views of this house and property. It was probably located in Chatsworth, possibly along Andora Avenue.

# APPENDIX A

# EPISODE GUIDE
## In Broadcast Order

**Season 1** (with filming dates, where known)

Road-Block aka Prison Break (filmed April 11-13, 1955)
Machine-Napping aka Machine Story (filmed August 22-24, 1955)
Reckless Driving (filmed August 19-20, 1955)
Lookout (filmed August 25-26, 1955)
Gambling (filmed August 27-29, 1955)
Hitchhiker (filmed September 1-2, 1955)
Desert Town (filmed September 6-7, 1955)
Radioactive (filmed September 22-23, 1955)
Reformed Criminal (filmed September 13-14, 1955)
Father Thief (filmed September 15-16, 1955)
Retired Gangster (filmed September 20-21, 1955)
Phony Insurance (filmed September 26-27, 1955)
Escort (filmed August 30-31, 1955)
Resort (filmed October 3-4, 1955)
Girl Bandit (filmed October 11-12, 1955)
Mountain-Copter (filmed October 25-27, 1955)
Lie Detector (filmed October 15-17, 1955)
Scared Cop (filmed October 24-25, 1955)
Harbor Story
Hit and Run (filmed October 30-November 1, 1955)
Car Theft (filmed November 3-4, 1955)
Human Bomb (filmed November 5-7, 1955)
Plane Crash (filmed November 10-11, 1955)
Desert-Copter (filmed November 15-17, 1955)
Plant Robbery (filmed November 21-22, 1955)
Released Convict (filmed November 30-December 1, 1955)
Motorcycle (filmed December 7-8, 1955)
Mental Patient (filmed December 14-15, 1955)
License Plates (filmed December 19-21, 1955)
Hitchhiker Dies (filmed December 27-28, 1955)
Blast Area-Copter (filmed February 20-22, 1956)
Anti-toxin (filmed February 23-24, 1956)
Dead Patrolman (filmed February 27-28, 1956)
Art Robbery (filmed February 29-March 1, 1956)
Runaway Boy (filmed February 9-10, 1956)
Taxi
Missing Witness (filmed March 12-14, 1956)
Prospector
Christmas Story (filmed September 30-October 1, 1955)

**Season 2**

The Search

Kidnap-Copter
Trailer Story
Fisherman's Luck
Magazine Writer
Typhoid Carrier
Hot Rod
Hot Cargo
Oil Lease
Ex-Con
Motel Robbery
Stolen Car Ring
Escaped Mental Patient
Armored Car
Migrant Workers
Ranch-Copter
Amnesia
Statute of Limitations
Resident Officer
Psycho
Counterfeit
Suspected Cop
Trojan Horse
Female Hitchhiker
Nitro
Motorcycle
Officer's Wife
Stripped Cars
Convict's Wife
Reformation
Stolen Plane-Copter
Gem Robbery
Wounded
Fake Cop
Double Cross
Narcotics
Hired Killer
Hostage-Copter
Rabies

## Season 3

Hypo Bandit
Efficiency Secretary
Temptation
Safecracker
Mistaken Identity
Hostage Family Copter
The Sniper
Hot Dust

Witness Wife
Dead Hunter
Convicted Innocent
Chain Store
Double Death
Hideout
Mother's March
Slain Cabby
Insulin
The 7th Green
Foster Child
Lady Bandits
Revenge
Tear Gas Copter
Deaf Mute
Hit and Run
Fear
Careless Cop
Policewoman
The Truckers
Credit Card
Psycho-Killer
Suicide
Phony Cop
The Judge
Dan's Vacation
Explosives
Hostage Officer
Double Copter
Dan's Sick
Reward

**Season 4**

Frightened Witness
Hostage
Family Affair
Transmitter Danger
Gambling Story
Train Copter
Portrait of Death
Train Robbery
Deadly Diamonds
Blood Money
False Confession
Confidence Game
Split Robbery
The Trap
Expose

Breath of a Child
Narcotics Racket
Copter Cave In
Gem Robbery
Mexican Chase
Framed Cop
The Collector
Revenge
Brave Boy
Diversion Robbery
Cargo Hi Jack
Hitch Hiker
Illegal Entry
Killer on the Run
Prisoner Exchange Copter
Dan Hostage
Woman Escapes
Auto Press
Express Delivery
Desperate Men
Confession
Detour to Death
Fire
Bank Messenger

NOTE: This listing uses the episode names as found in the U.S. Copyright Office records.

# EPISODE GUIDE
### Alphabetical Order
### With Locations

*Amnesia*
Griffith Park Boy's Camp, Los Angeles

*Anti-Toxin*
NW corner of Topanga Canyon Bl and Avenue San Luis, Woodland Hills
Peterson Dairy Farm, 9409 Farralone Ave, Chatsworth

*Armored Car*
Shermart Market, 8840 Santa Monica Bl, Los Angeles
8841 Santa Monica Bl, Los Angeles
Paul's Radio Service, 8870 Santa Monica Bl, Los Angeles
Hotel, 8869 Santa Monica Bl, Los Angeles
1165 Poinsettia Pl, Los Angeles
Mountain Patrol Fire Station 2, 16500 Mulholland Dr, Encino

*Art Robbery*
Bernadine Apartments, 2402 N Beachwood Dr, Los Angeles
Apartments, 2438 N Beachwood Dr, Los Angeles
2328 N Beachwood Dr, Los Angeles
House, 2420 N Beachwood Dr, Los Angeles
Bronson Canyon, Los Angeles

*Auto Press*
Mulholland Dr and Roscomare Rd, Los Angeles
701 E 222nd St., Carson

*Bank Messenger*
Lookout Mountain, Los Angeles
Chavez Ravine, Los Angeles
Mayo Motel, 841 N Figueroa St, now 903 New Depot St, Los Angeles
Stadium Way Freeway Underpass, Los Angeles
Brownie Letter Shop (City Bank), 1751 Hillhurst Ave, Los Angeles
800 Block of Centennial St, Los Angeles
NE Corner of Centennial St and New Depot, Los Angeles
ZIV Studio, Los Angeles

*Blast Area-Copter*
Jim Woolvin Richfield Gas Station, 2694 N Beachwood Dr, Los Angeles
Bronson Canyon, Los Angeles

*Blood Money*
Southern Pacific Taylor Yard, Los Angeles
Stadium Way and Boylston St, Los Angeles
Former Cedars of Lebanon Hospital (now Scientology), 4833 Fountain Ave, Los Angeles

**Brave Boy**
1541 N Ogden Dr, Los Angeles
across from 1549 N Ogden Dr, Los Angeles
Hal Jaffe Auto Repair, 7601 Santa Monica Bl, Los Angeles
1609 N Ogden Dr, Los Angeles
1623 N Ogden Dr, Los Angeles
1120 N Curson Ave, Los Angeles
1629 N Ogden Dr, Los Angeles
Genesee Ave and Ogden Ave, Los Angeles
alley north of Santa Monica Bl between Spaulding Ave and Curson Ave, Los Angeles
Courtney Ave and Hollywood Blvd, Los Angeles
7758 Sunset Blvd, Los Angeles
Selma Ave and Courtney Ave, Los Angeles

**Breath of a Child**
Upper Franklin Canyon Reservoir, Beverly Hills
South house at dam at Upper Franklin Canyon Reservoir, Beverly Hills
Upper house at Upper Franklin Canyon Reservoir, Beverly Hills

**Careless Cop**
Four Oaks Restaurant, 2181 N Beverly Glen Bl, Los Angeles
Exterior ZIV Studio, N Fuller Ave, Los Angeles
ZIV Studio, Los Angeles

**Cargo Hi Jack**
Griffith Park near Golf Academy Entrance, Los Angeles
Poinsettia Place and Romaine St, Los Angeles
ZIV Studio, Los Angeles

**Car Theft**
Frosty's Towing, 3924 W El Segundo Bl, Hawthorne
Building, 3940 W El Segundo Bl, Hawthorne
Seers Lumber, 3856 W El Segundo Bl, Hawthorne
Buildings on SE corner, W. El Segundo Bl and Roselle Av, Hawthorne
House, near 608 Washington Blvd, now a parking lot, Marina del Rey

**Chain Store**
Wilshire Food Center, 214 N Larchmont Bl, Los Angeles
Behind Wilshire Food Center, 214 N Larchmont Bl, Los Angeles
531 N Lucerne Bl, Los Angeles
Lucerne Bl and 1st St, Los Angeles
NW Lucerne Bl and W 1st St, Los Angeles
W 1st St and Arden Bl, Los Angeles
Larchmont Travel Agency, 221 Larchmont Bl, Los Angeles
S Beachwood Dr and W 2nd St, Los Angeles

**Christmas Story**
Brentwood Motor Hotel, 12200 W Sunset Bl, Los Angeles
PerryGraf Slide-Chart, 150 S Barrington Av, Los Angeles

104 S Medio Dr, Los Angeles
Sunset Bl east from Medio Dr, Los Angeles

## The Collector
2633 Canyon Dr, Los Angeles
House, corner Foothill Dr and N Bronson Av, Los Angeles
Apartment, corner Foothill Dr and Canyon Dr, Los Angeles
Bronsonia Pharmacy, 5889 Franklin Ave, Los Angeles
Alley between Bronson Ave, Canyon Dr, Carlton Way, and Harold Way, Los Angeles

## Confession
The Liquor House, 8834 Reseda Bl, Northridge
Medical Building, 8833 Reseda Bl, Northridge
Johnny's Shoe Service, 8831 Reseda Bl, Northridge
Realty Office, 8830 Reseda Bl, Northridge
Bernard Grossman, Attorney at Law, 8829 Reseda Bl, Northridge
8883 Reseda Bl, Northridge
8900 Reseda Bl, Northridge
Church Building, Gresham St at alley between Reseda Bl and Baird Av, Northridge
Vanalden Ave and Kinzie St, Northridge
between Tampa Ave and Vanalden Ave, north of Plummer St, Northridge
Kinzie St and Beckford Av, Northridge

## Confidence Game
802 Centennial St, Los Angeles
Loma Linda Elementary School, Effie St and Paducah St, Los Angeles
Chavez Ravine, Los Angeles
City Center Grocery Store, 1146 Effie St, Los Angeles
House, 1205 Effie St, Los Angeles

## Convicted Innocent
Gas Station, 1200 N Virgil Ave, Los Angeles
1215 N Virgil Ave, Los Angeles
House, 4453 Lexington Ave, Los Angeles
House, 4455 Lexington Ave, Los Angeles
House, 4457 Lexington Ave, Los Angeles
Griffith Park, Los Angeles

## Convict's Wife
1233 Poinsettia Dr, Los Angeles
Poinsettia Dr and Hampton Ave, Los Angeles
Griffith Park, Los Angeles
Griffith Park Coffee Shop, Park Center, Los Angeles
Griffith Park Pony Ride, Los Angeles
Griffith Park Collidge Golf Course, Los Angeles
ZIV Studio, Los Angeles

## Copter Cave In
Mountain Patrol Fire Station 2, 16500 Mulholland Dr, Encino

Bronson Canyon, Los Angeles

*Counterfeit*
Harper Method Approved Shop, 143 N Larchmont Bl, Los Angeles
Earl Hays Press, 1121 Las Palmas, Los Angeles
130 block of N Larchmont Bl, Los Angeles
W. H. Wilshire Studios, 103 N Larchmont Bl, Los Angeles
McCarthy Gift Shop, 161 N Larchmont Bl, Los Angeles
Landis Department Store, 157 N Larchmont Bl, Los Angeles
Myrts Corner Hamburger Stand, 7350 Melrose Ave, Los Angeles
Melrose Market, 7355 Melrose Ave, Los Angeles
alley from Romaine St to Willoughby Ave between Highland Ave and Citrus Ave, Los Angeles
NW corner building, south side, Willoughby Ave at Highland, Los Angeles
Apartments, 6815 Willoughby Ave, Los Angeles
Apartments, 6851 Willoughby Ave, Los Angeles

*Credit Card*
Harry E. McConnell Service Station, 1000 N Alvarado St, Los Angeles
Chavez Ravine, Los Angeles
ZIV Studio, Los Angeles

*Dan Hostage*
House, 1205 Effie St, Los Angeles
Chavez Ravine, Los Angeles

*Dan Sick*
9857 Vanalden Ave, Northridge

*Dan's Vacation*
Mick's Grill, 8322 Reseda Bl, Northridge
Griffith Park Boy's Camp, Los Angeles

*Dead Hunter*
4459 Gainsborough Ave, Los Angeles
City Center Grocery Store, 1146 Effie St, Los Angeles
Chavez Ravine, Los Angeles
1720 Hillhurst Ave, Los Angeles
1701 Hillhurst Ave, Los Angeles
DWP, 1675 Hillhurst Ave, Los Angeles
SE corner Hillhurst Ave and Prospect Ave, Los Angeles

*Dead Patrolman*
7327 Melrose Ave
Nielsen's Books, 7308 Melrose Ave, Los Angeles
Alley behind 7308 Melrose Ave, Los Angeles
Corner Melrose Ave and Fuller Ave, Los Angeles
Nichols Canyon Rd and Del Zuro Dr, Los Angeles
Nichols Canyon Rd and La Cuesta Dr, Los Angeles
Novelty Quilting, 7373 Melrose Ave, Los Angeles

Danny's Used Cars, 501 N La Brea Ave, Los Angeles

**Deadly Diamonds**
Victory Motel, 15052 Ventura Bl, Los Angeles
Colfax Cleaners, 4360 Coldwater Canyon Ave, Los Angeles

**Deaf Mute**
City Center Grocery Store, 1146 Effie St, Los Angeles
Effie St and Reposa St, Los Angeles
House, 1205 Effie St, Los Angeles
Chavez Ravine, Los Angeles

**Desert-Copter**
South of 34278 Cheseboro Rd, Palmdale
Cheseboro Rd and Mt Emma Rd, Palmdale

**Desert Town**
29001 Agoura Rd, Agoura
Seminole Hot Springs Inn, 29008 Agoura Rd, Agoura
Ranch on hill, Marin St, Thousand Oaks

**Desperate Men**
Dr Theodore T Alexander Jr Science Center, Exposition Park, 3980 Bill Robertson Ln, Los
   Angeles
Exposition Park, 3980 Bill Robertson Ln, Los Angeles
ZIV Studio, Los Angeles

**Detour to Death**
Mountain Patrol Fire Station 2, 16500 Mulholland Dr, Encino

**Diversion Robbery**
4529 Sylmar Ave, Sherman Oaks
Sherman Oaks Jewelers, 14522 Ventura Bl, Sherman Oaks
Mountain Patrol Fire Station 2, 16500 Mulholland Dr, Encino
Nahas Department Store, 4520 Van Nuys Bl, Sherman Oaks
Sylmar Palms Apartments, 4555 Sylmar Ave, Sherman Oaks

**Double Copter**
Mountain Patrol Fire Station 2, 16500 Mulholland Dr, Encino

**Double Cross**
Escrow Guarantee, 13900 Ventura Bl, Sherman Oaks
Tropi Kool Pools, 13865 Ventura Bl, Sherman Oaks
Maple Leaf Motel, 13901 Ventura Bl, Sherman Oaks
4101 Stansbury Ave, Sherman Oaks
Stansbury Ave and Roblar Rd, Sherman Oaks
Behind 13900 Ventura Bl, Sherman Oaks

### Double Death
4301 Parva Ave, Los Angeles
CHP Headquarters (office building) 1662 Hillhurst Ave, Los Angeles
Dept of Water and Power Distributing Station, 1675 Hillhurst Ave, Los Angeles
East side of intersection, Hillhurst Ave and Price, Los Angeles
Apartments, 1822 Hillhurst Ave, Los Angeles
1200 N Virgil Ave, Los Angeles
E. D. Cristman Real Estate, 1863 Hillhurst Ave, Los Angeles
Hillhurst Mart, 2060 Hillhurst Ave, Los Angeles
Ise's Automotive Service, 1774 Hillhurst Ave, Los Angeles
3660 Amesbury Rd, Los Angeles
Apartment, 2105 N Commonwealth Ave, Los Angeles
House, 2115 N Commonwealth Ave, Los Angeles
Apartment, 2121 N Commonwealth Ave, Los Angeles
Traveling Shot, looking north from 2105 N Commonwealth Ave, Los Angeles

### Efficiency Secretary
Whiteman Airport, Los Angeles
4 Chimneys near intersection of S. San Fernando Bl and Sheldon St, Pacoima
Looking NE beyond Hansen Dam, Pacoima

### Escaped Mental Patient
Upper Franklin Canyon Reservoir, Beverly Hills
Lower house, Upper Franklin Canyon Reservoir, Beverly Hills
Franklin Canyon Dr and Beverly Pl, Beverly Hills
House, 1845 Franklin Canyon Dr, Beverly Hills
House, 1853 Franklin Canyon Dr, Beverly Hills

### Escort
San Fernando Jr High Auditorium, 130 N Brand Bl, San Fernando
638 San Fernando Rd at Ilex St, San Fernando
Mayfair Market, 1320 San Fernando Rd, San Fernando
Community Park, 208 Park Ave, San Fernando
House, 24317 N Newhall Av, Newhall
Foothill Blvd near Balboa Blvd, Los Angeles
Foothill Blvd near Filbert St, Los Angeles
San Fernando Rd under Golden State Freeway, Los Angeles

### Ex Con
Gas Station and House, 10124 Topanga Canyon Bl, Chatsworth
Chatsworth Reservoir, near 23236 Valley Circle Bl, Chatsworth

### Explosives
1609 N Genesee Ave, Los Angeles
Nichols Canyon, Los Angeles
Mulholland Dr and Torreyson Dr, Los Angeles
near 2533 Nichols Canyon Rd, Los Angeles
ZIV Studio, Los Angeles

## Expose
Maple Leaf Motel, 13901 Ventura Bl, Sherman Oaks
3755 Longridge Ave, Sherman Oaks
4645 Van Nuys Bl, Sherman Oaks
Park Seville Apartments, 14065 Moorpark St, Sherman Oaks
HP Headquarters, 5539 Van Nuys Bl, Sherman Oaks
NW corner of Longridge Ave and Ethel Ave, Sherman Oaks
3655 Longridge Ave, Sherman Oaks

## Express Delivery
Southern Pacific Glendale Train Station, Glendale
Central Motel, 1516 S Central Ave, Glendale
1729 Gardena Ave, Glendale
Los Feliz Bl and San Fernando Rd, Glendale
Cerritos Ave, Glendale
San Fernando Rd and Cerritos Ave, Glendale

## Fake Cop
Shopping Cart, 21360 Devonshire St, Chatsworth
Chatsworth Cleaners, 21824 Devonshire, Chatsworth
Gas Station, 10124 Topanga Canyon Bl, Chatsworth
Topanga Canyon Bl and Andora Ave, Chatsworth
Devonshire St and Andora Ave, Chatsworth

## False Confession
N Beaudry Ave near Figueroa Terrace, Los Angeles
Figueroa Terrace and W College St, Los Angeles
871 Figueroa Terrace, Los Angeles
Figueroa Terrace and Pasadena Fwy Exit, Los Angeles
Alpine St and White Knoll Dr, Los Angeles
Paradise Motel, 1116 Sunset Bl, Los Angeles
Gas Station, 1106 Sunset Bl, Los Angeles
Backyards between 960 and 966 Everett St, Los Angeles
1148 Alpine St, Los Angeles
Alley off Alpine St between Beaudry Ave and White Knoll Dr, Los Angeles
Stadium Way and Boylston St, Los Angeles
1043 Alpine St, Los Angeles
Alley west of 1148 Alpine St, Los Angeles

## Family Affair
Barlow Hospital, 2000 Stadium Way, Los Angeles
House, Davis St, Los Angeles
Chavez Ravine, Los Angeles

## Father Thief
(NOTE: E. Thousand Oaks Blvd used to be Ventura Blvd)
2974 E Thousand Oaks Bl, Thousand Oaks
rear 2860 E Thousand Oaks Bl, Thousand Oaks
Max & Rose Cafe, 3006 E Thousand Oaks Bl, Thousand Oaks

Junior Department Store, 3021 E Thousand Oaks Bl, Thousand Oaks
Conejo Pharmacy, 3041 E Thousand Oaks Bl, Thousand Oaks
2884 Crescent Way, Thousand Oaks

## Fear
Chavez Ravine, Los Angeles
ZIV Studio, Los Angeles

## Fire
Southern Pacific Northridge Train Station, Northridge
Allen's Market, 8738 Reseda Bl, Northridge
Northridge Lumber Co, 8703 Reseda Bl, Northridge
possibly between Bothwell Rd Melvin Av Citronia St Ballinger St, Northridge

## Female Hitchhiker
Apartments, 10727 Balboa Bl, Granada Hills
Spudnutt Shop, 10705 Balboa Bl, Granada Hills
Houses, 10718 to 10732 Balboa Bl, Granada Hills
Tulsa St, Chatsworth
Farralone St, Chatsworth

## Fisherman's Luck
Upper Franklin Canyon Reservoir, Beverly Hills
Lower house, Upper Franklin Canyon Reservoir, Beverly Hills
ZIV Studio, Los Angeles

## Foster Child
House, 1226 Lilac Pl, Los Angeles
House, 1232 Lilac Pl, Los Angeles
Elysian Park Old Lodge, Los Angeles

## Framed Cop
3465 Rowena Ave, Los Angeles
4150 Los Feliz Bl, Los Angeles
3472 Rowena Ave, Los Angeles
3126 Los Feliz Bl, Los Angeles
Tam O'Shanter Inn, 2980 Los Feliz Bl, Los Angeles
Hillhurst Market, 2060 Hillhurst Ave, Los Angeles
Southern Pacific Glendale Train Station, Glendale
East side background, Hillhurst Ave and Finley, Los Angeles
East side intersection, Hillhurst Ave and Price, Los Angeles
Los Feliz Hotel, 3101 Los Feliz Bl, Los Angeles
Los Feliz Bl and Perlita Ave, Los Angeles

## Frightened Witness
29001 Agoura Rd, Agoura
Motel next to 26300 Ventura Bl, Calabasas
Seminole Hot Springs Inn, 29008 Agoura Rd, Agoura
Agoura Stock Farm, west of Cornell Rd, Agoura

ZIV Studio, Los Angeles

## *Gambling*
Ventura Bl and Alhama Dr, Woodland Hills
Pacific Lodge Youth Services, 4900 Serrania Av, Woodland Hills
Dumetz Rd at Serrania Ave, Woodland Hills
North side of Woodland Hills Golf Course, Ibanez Ave, Woodland Hills
Calabasas Rd just west of Sperling Nursery, Calabasas
Calabasas Rd east of Mureau Rd, Calabasas
Hwy 101 east of Mureau Rd, Calabasas

## *Gambling Story*
NE corner of Melrose Ave and Genesee Ave, Los Angeles
728 Genesee Ave, Los Angeles
7710 Melrose Ave, Los Angeles
NW corner of Melrose and Spaulding Ave, Los Angeles
740 Spaulding Ave, Los Angeles

## *Gem Robbery* (Season 2)
Southern Pacific Glendale Train Station, Glendale
Fern Dell, Los Angeles
ZIV Studio, Los Angeles

## *Gem Robbery* (Season 4)
Southern Pacific Glendale Train Station, Glendale
Bank of America, San Fernando Rd and W. Cerritos Ave, Glendale
The Maple Shop, 206 W Los Feliz Rd, Glendale
Mira Loma Ave and Gardena Ave, Glendale
1729 Gardena Ave, Glendale

## *Girl Bandit*
Saugus Speedway, 22500 Soledad Canyon Rd, Saugus
House, 24317 N Newhall Av, Newhall
915 Citrus Ave, Los Angeles
N Fuller Ave next ZIV Studio, Los Angeles
Saugus Cafe, 25861 Railroad Ave, Santa Clarita
Joe Hran Texaco, SE corner Sierra Hwy and Soledad Canyon Rd, Saugus
Log Cabin Motel, SE corner Sierra Hwy and Soledad Canyon Rd, Saugus
NW corner building, south side, Willoughby at Highland, Los Angeles
NE corner building, south side, 900 Highland Ave, Los Angeles
SW corner, Willoughby and Alley west of Highland Ave, Los Angeles

## *Harbor Story*
15301 Antioch St, Pacific Palisades
15322 Antioch St, Pacific Palisades
15328 Antioch St, Pacific Palisades
alley between 15317 Antioch St and 910 Via De La Paz, Pacific Palisades
Civic Center Way and Malibu Canyon Rd, Malibu
Civic Center Way along PCH, Malibu

Paradise Cove and Pier, 28128 Pacific Coast Hwy, Malibu

## Hideout
City Center Grocery Store, 1146 Effie St, Los Angeles
House, 1205 Effie St, Los Angeles
Los Angeles Police Academy, 1880 Academy Dr, Los Angeles

## Hired Killer
Southern Pacific Chatsworth Train Station, Chatsworth
Cabin Cafe, 20852 Devonshire St, Chatsworth
Elizabeth's Cafe, 21754 Devonshire St, Chatsworth
Mountain Patrol Fire Station 2, 16500 Mulholland Dr, Encino

## Hit and Run (Season 1)
12755 Culver Bl, Los Angeles
12961 Panama St, Los Angeles
12900 block Panama St, Los Angeles
Ballona Creek Bridge, Overland Ave, Culver City
Farm, near Hughes Airport, now under water in Marina Del Rey, just north of Palawan Way

## Hit and Run (Season 3)
Pacific Electric Sherman Yard, 8800 Santa Monica Bl, West Los Angeles
House, 628 N Westbourne Dr, West Los Angeles
Sunset Tower Hotel, 9358 Sunset Bl, West Los Angeles

## Hitchhiker
House, 10320 Hillview Av, Chatsworth
Building, 21800 Devonshire St, Chatsworth
Building, 21757 Devonshire St, Chatsworth
Building, 21743 Devonshire St, Chatsworth
Topanga Canyon Bl, north towards Parthenia St, Chatsworth
Topanga Canyon Bl, south towards Plummer St, Chatsworth
A & B Motors, 19326 Ventura Bl, Los Angeles
ZIV Studio, Los Angeles

## Hitch Hiker
Elysian Park Adaptive Recreation Center, 835 Academy Rd, Los Angeles
Lilac Terrace, west of 110 Freeway, Los Angeles
Lilac Terrace, Naval and Marine Corps Reserve Center in background at 1700 Stadium Way, Los Angeles
Lookout Mountain, Chavez Ravine, Los Angeles

## Hitchhiker Dies
1233 Greenacre Ave, Los Angeles
Forest Lawn Drive, Burbank
4439 Lakeside Dr, Burbank
South on Fuller Ave to Romaine St, Los Angeles
CHP Headquarters, 936 Poinsettia Pl, Los Angeles
ZIV Studio, Los Angeles

## Hostage

Southern Pacific Glendale Train Station, Glendale
Cerritos Ave and Gardena Ave, Glendale
Central Ave and Railroad St, Glendale
1681 S Central Ave, Glendale
3704 Dover St, Glendale
Dover St and Brunswick Ave, Glendale
3700 Dover St, Glendale
Club Tee Yee, 3208 Glendale Bl, Los Angeles
Building, 3210 Glendale Bl, Los Angeles
Building, 3212 Glendale Bl, Los Angeles
Safeway Market, 3080 Glendale Bl, Glendale

## Hostage-Copter

Mulholland Dr and Encino Hills, Encino
Mountain Patrol Fire Station 2, 16500 Mulholland Dr, Encino

## Hostage Family Copter

Mountain Patrol Fire Station 2, 16500 Mulholland Dr, Encino

## Hostage Officer

Davis St, Los Angeles
Davis St and Giraldi St, Los Angeles
Chavez Ravine, Los Angeles

## Hot Cargo

Mountain Patrol Fire Station 2, 16500 Mulholland Dr, Encino
922 N Formosa Ave, Los Angeles
Ad-Type, 916 N Formosa Ave, Los Angeles
941 N Formosa Ave, Los Angeles
NW corner Formosa Ave and Willoughby Ave, Los Angeles
NE corner Formosa Ave and Willoughby Ave, Los Angeles
SE corner Formosa Ave and Romaine St, Los Angeles

## Hot Dust

Fern Dell, Los Angeles
ZIV Studio, Los Angeles

## Hot Rod

Chuck's Fountain & Grill, 8257 Winnetka Ave, Canoga Park
Bill's Market, 20059 Roscoe Bl, Canoga Park
Jebs Restaurant, 7600 Balboa Bl, Van Nuys
Monahan's Inn, 16848 Saticoy, Van Nuys
9857 Vanalden Ave, Northridge
20851 Roscoe Bl, Winnetka

## Human Bomb

Seminole Hot Springs Inn, 29008 Agoura Rd, Agoura
Storage Tank on Formosa near Santa Monica Bl, Los Angeles

Garage behind 13629 Ventura Bl, Sherman Oaks
4321 Ventura Canyon Ave, Sherman Oaks
Bronson Canyon, Canyon Drive, Los Angeles

*Hypo Bandit*
Lehrer Fine Furs, 1167 N Western Ave, Los Angeles
Eugene's Jewelers, 1745 N Vermont Ave, Los Angeles
Colt Ventilation of America Inc., 4652 Hollywood Bl, Los Angeles
Andrews Window Shade & Floor Covering Co, 1175 N Western Ave, Los Angeles
W. O. Renman Electrical Contractor, 4655 Hollywood Bl, Los Angeles
Richfield Service Station, 4696 Hollywood Bl, Los Angeles
Griffith Park Vermont Ave entrance, Los Angeles
Mountain Patrol Fire Station 2, 16500 Mulholland Dr, Encino

*Illegal Entry*
Elysian Park Adaptive Recreation Center, 835 Academy Rd, Los Angeles
Chavez Ravine, Los Angeles
ZIV Studio, Los Angeles

*Insulin*
2245 Canyon Dr, Los Angeles
corner Canyon Dr and Bronson Hill Dr, Los Angeles
Bronson Canyon, Los Angeles

*The Judge*
Elysian Park Ave at Lilac Pl, Los Angeles
House, 1226 Lilac Pl, Los Angeles
House, 1233 Lilac Pl, Los Angeles
Apartment, next door (right) to 1233 Lilac Pl, Los Angeles
Lilac Terrace, Naval and Marine Corps Reserve Center in background at 1700 Stadium Way, Los Angeles
ZIV Studio, Los Angeles

*Kidnap-Copter*
2727 Benedict Canyon Dr, Los Angeles

*Killer on the Run*
Stone Printing Co, 681 Spaulding Ave, Los Angeles
TraveLodge, 7370 Sunset Bl, Los Angeles
Young Israel, 660 N Spaulding Ave, Los Angeles
DeLongpre Park, 1350 N Cherokee Ave, Los Angeles
Apartments, 1340 N June St, Los Angeles
Mulholland Dr and Torreyson Dr, Los Angeles
William C Jagy Service Station, 7253 Melrose Ave, Los Angeles
Gene's Auto Works, 7229 Melrose Ave, Los Angeles
2615 Harlesden Ct, Los Angeles
Willow Glen Rd and Harlesden Ct, Los Angeles
Willow Glen and Woodstock, Los Angeles
possibly Nichols Canyon and Willow Glen, Los Angeles

**Lady Bandits**
Joe Tommaso Market, 1041 Alpine St, Los Angeles
corner Centennial St and Alpine St, Los Angeles
D. N. Nicassio Real Estate, 802 Centennial St, Los Angeles
Lilac Terrace and Chavez Ravine Rd, Los Angeles
Chavez Ravine, Los Angeles
ZIV Studio, Los Angeles

**License Plates**
Furniture Store, 907 N Hollywood Way, Burbank
American Lutheran Church, 755 N Whitnall Hwy, Burbank
Kirk's Drug Store, 817 N Hollywood Way, Burbank
Alley from N Hollywood Way to N Screenland Dr, Burbank
814 N Screenland Dr, Burbank
815 N Screenland Dr, Burbank
819 N Screenland Dr, Burbank
823 N Screenland Dr, Burbank (all houses 823 and south to corner)
SW and NE corner of W Clark Av and N Screenland Dr, Burbank
Traveling Shot, Clark Ave between Kenwood St and Screenland Dr (south side), Burbank
Hollywood Police Station, 1358 Wilcox Ave, Los Angeles
Jerry McGurrin, Realtor, 3711 Clark Ave, Burbank
Starlite Lodge, 3320 W Olive Ave, Burbank

**Lie Detector**
San Fernando Valley Motel, 7533 Sepulveda Bl, Van Nuys
Deeks Realty, 7500 Sepulveda Bl, Van Nuys
Real Estate, 7246 Sepulveda Bl, Van Nuys

**Lookout**
Restaurant, 15603 Hawthrone Bl, Lawndale
Library Park, Palm Ave and Richmond St, El Segundo
near Flight View Restaurant, 310 E Imperial Ave, El Segundo
Apartments, 548 W Imperial Ave, El Segundo
600 block W Imperial Ave, El Segundo
854 Hillcrest St, El Segundo
Walnut Ave and Hillcrest St, El Segundo

**Machine-Napping**
San Fernando Rd and Brand Bl, San Fernando
Hotel Goodhap, 208 Brand Bl, San Fernando
Bank, 1148 San Fernando Rd, San Fernando
Corner San Fernando Mission Rd and Celis St, San Fernando
Corner Brand Boulevard and Celis St, San Fernando
Safeway Market, 1212 Celis St, San Fernando
Helms Pontiac-Cadillac, 1212 San Fernando Rd, San Fernando
Griffith Park Tunnel, both east and west entrances, Los Angeles
ZIV Studio, Los Angeles

**Magazine Writer**
Mountain Patrol Fire Station 2, 16500 Mulholland Dr, Encino
15433 Mulholland Dr, Los Angeles

**Mental Patient**
Chatsworth Reservoir, Valley Circle Bl west of Plummer St, Chatsworth
Peterson Dairy Farm, 9409 Farralone Ave, Chatsworth
Plummer St at Hanna Ave, Chatsworth
Plummer St at Topanga Canyon Pl, Chatsworth

**Mexican Chase**
Mountain Patrol Fire Station 2, 16500 Mulholland Dr, Encino
Mulholland Dr west of 16500 Mulholland Dr, Encino
The Overlook, across street from 16500 Mulholland Dr, Encino

**Migrant Workers**
Mountain Patrol Fire Station 2, 16500 Mulholland Dr, Encino

**Missing Witness**
936 N Poinsettia Pl, Los Angeles
Ross Cleaners, 1708 N. Bronson Av, Los Angeles
2707 Canyon Dr, Los Angeles
Entrance to Bronson Canyon, Los Angeles
Bronson Canyon, Los Angeles

**Mistaken Identity**
Maple Leaf Motel, 13901 Ventura Bl, Sherman Oaks
Rand's Ventura Round-Up, 13920 Ventura Bl, Sherman Oaks
Ventura Bl and Stern Ave, Sherman Oaks
Mulholland Dr and Franklin Canyon, Beverly Hills

**Motel Robbery**
Panorama Motel, 8209 Sepulveda Bl, Van Nuys
Rita Curtis Swim School, 8220 Sepulveda Bl, Van Nuys
Monticello Hotel, 8071 Sepulveda Bl, Van Nuys
Saticoy St and Gaynor Av, Van Nuys
Busch Brewery, Roscoe Bl and Haskell Av, Van Nuys

**Mother's March**
2800 N Beachwood Dr, Los Angeles
2836 N Beachwood Dr, Los Angeles
2838 N Beachwood Dr, Los Angeles
Hill-Top Beauty Salon, 2691 N Beachwood Dr, Los Angeles
Alley on side of 2691 N Beachwood Dr, Los Angeles
Alley exit between 2673 and 2677 N Beachwood Dr, Los Angeles
Beachwood Dr towards Glen Oak, Los Angeles

**Motorcycle** (Season 1)
Chatsworth Market, 10249 Topanga Canyon Bl, Chatsworth

Town & Country Cafe, 10255 Topanga Canyon Bl, Chatsworth
9754 Topanga Canyon Bl, Chatsworth
Topanga Canyon Bl and Marilla St, Chatsworth
ZIV Studio, Los Angeles

*Motorcycle* (Season 2)
Mountain Patrol Fire Station 2, 16500 Mulholland Dr, Encino
15341 Mulholland Dr, Los Angeles

*Mountain-Copter*
Griffith Park Boy's Camp, Los Angeles

*Narcotics*
Cabin Cafe, 20852 Devonshire St, Chatsworth
Street towards north, 9644 DeSoto Av, Chatsworth
Street with house in background, DeSoto Av above Rinaldi, Chatsworth

*Narcotics Racket*
Mick's Grill, 8322 Reseda Bl, Northridge
Huckins Steaks, 17301 Ventura Bl, Encino
Encino Oaks Motor Lodge, 17323 Ventura Bl, Encino
Walter D. Bigg Jeweler, 8827 Reseda Bl, Northridge
8814 Reseda Bl, Northridge
Marilla St near Vanalden Ave, Northridge

*Nitro*
Mountain Patrol Fire Station 2, 16500 Mulholland Dr, Encino

*Officer's Wife*
2243 Canyon Dr, Los Angeles
Runyon Park, Mulholland Dr and Runyon Canyon Rd, Los Angeles

*Oil Lease*
Baldwin Hills Oil Field, Culver City
Mulholland Dr from 16500 to west, Encino

*Phony Cop*
Building, 5150 Babcock Ave, Valley Village
5439 Coldwater Canyon, Valley Village
Nursery, possibly 12920 Magnolia Bl, Valley Village

*Phony Insurance*
Dr. R. L. Snow, 7125 Darby Ave, Reseda
Grand Central Warehouse, 7115 Darby Ave, Reseda
Building, 7131 Darby Ave, Reseda
Anita, 18361 Sherman Wy, Reseda
Lawson Jewelers, 18353 Sherman Wy, Reseda
Building, SW corner Darby Ave and Gault St, Reseda
29001 Agoura Rd, Agoura

Seminole Hot Springs Inn, 29008 Agoura Rd, Agoura

**Plane Crash**
Iverson Movie Ranch, Santa Susana Pass Rd, Chatsworth

**Plant Robbery**
Shermart Market, 8840 Santa Monica Bl, Los Angeles
California Super Service Gas Station, 8797 Santa Monica Bl, Los Angeles
Kay & Art's Cafe, 8785 Santa Monica Bl, Los Angeles
Ervin's Auto Wrecking, 8775 Santa Monica Bl, Los Angeles
ZIV Studio, Los Angeles

**Policewoman**
Fern Dell, Los Angeles

**Portrait of Death**
Four Oaks Restaurant, 2181 N Beverly Glen Blvd, Los Angeles
Apartments, 10403 Eastborne Ave, Los Angeles
Apartments, 10407 Eastborne Ave, Los Angeles
Comstock Ave and Holman Ave, Los Angeles
Comstock Ave north from Santa Monica Bl, Los Angeles
Apartments, 1643 S Beverly Glen Bl, Los Angeles
1812 Holmby Ave, Los Angeles
10460 Santa Monica Bl, Los Angeles

**Prisoner Exchange Copter**
Seminole Hot Springs Inn, 29008 Agoura Rd, Agoura
29001 Agoura Rd, Agoura
Agoura Stock Farm, Agoura Rd west of Cornell Rd, Agoura
Bronson Canyon, Los Angeles

**Prospector**
Bronson Canyon, Los Angeles
1011 Fuller, Los Angeles
ZIV Studio, Los Angeles

**Psycho**
Lower Franklin Canyon Reservoir, Beverly Hills

**Psycho-Killer**
Upper Franklin Canyon Reservoir, Beverly Hills
Lower house, Upper Franklin Canyon Reservoir, Beverly Hills
Upper house, Upper Franklin Canyon Reservoir, Beverly Hills

**Rabies**
Texaco Service Station, 2707 Belden Dr, Los Angeles
Harrington Motel, 5224 Sunset Bl, Los Angeles
Griffith Park Boy's Camp Entrance Area, Los Angeles
Cafe (now The Trails), 2333 Fern Dell Dr, Los Angeles

3074 N Beachwood Dr, Los Angeles

### Radioactive
185 Culver Bl, Playa del Rey
200 Culver Bl, Playa del Rey
Nicholson St towards Culver Bl, Playa del Rey
5713 Eveward Rd, Culver City
corner Ranch Rd and Eveward Rd, Culver City
California Auto Parts & Wrecking Co, 9405 Jefferson Bl, Culver City
9425 Jefferson Bl, Culver City
across from 9425 Jefferson Bl, Culver City

### Ranch-Copter
Hilltop house, above intersection of Summitridge Dr and Beverly Park St, Beverly Hills

### Reckless Driving
Flight View Restaurant, 310 E Imperial Ave, El Segundo
Imperial Hwy next to LAX, Los Angeles
Vista del Mar next to Dockweiler Beach (smoke stack in background), Los Angeles
520 Main St, El Segundo
West side of 520 Main St (entire block towards north), El Segundo
Culver Bl crossing Ballona Creek eastward, Playa del Rey
Culver Bl east of Lincoln Bl, Playa del Rey

### Reformation
Griffith Park, Los Angeles
4451 Kingswell Ave, Los Angeles
Apartments, 4444-4450 Kingswell Ave, Los Angeles
1720 Hillhurst Ave, Los Angeles
1714 Hillhurst Ave, Los Angeles
4508 Finley Ave, Los Angeles
St. Mary of the Angels Episcopal Church, 4510 Finley Ave, Los Angeles
Union Oil Service Station, 2000 Hillhurst Ave, Los Angeles
Apartments, 4452 Finley Ave, Los Angeles
NW corner, Finley Ave and Hillhurst Ave, Los Angeles
Griffith Park Boy's Camp, Los Angeles

### Reformed Criminal
24347 Main St, Newhall
24359 Main St, Newhall
24355 Main St, Newhall
Paul Palmer, Attorney, 24369 Main St, Newhall
Cocktail Lounge, 24371 Main St, Newhall
Soledad Hotel, 24367 Main St, Newhall
Joe Hran Texaco, SE corner Sierra Hwy and Soledad Canyon Rd, Saugus

### Released Convict
Las Palmas Hotel, 1738 N Las Palmas Ave, Los Angeles, looking south towards First Baptist
  Church

Apartment, NE corner N Las Palmas Ave and Yucca St, Los Angeles
Apartment, 1749 N Las Palmas Ave, Los Angeles
Telephone booth, SE corner N Las Palmas Ave and Yucca St, Los Angeles
Chancellor Apartments, 1842 N Cherokee Ave, Los Angeles
Calatrana Dr and Medina Rd, Woodland Hills
Providencia St and Campo Rd, Woodland Hills
Dumetz Rd and Campo Rd, Woodland Hills
Ybarra Rd from Dumetz Rd, Woodland Hills
Dumetz Rd east of Campo Rd, Woodland Hills
Wishing Well Cafe, W 22941 Ventura Bl, Los Angeles

### Resident Officer
Gas Station, 10124 Topanga Canyon Bl, Chatsworth
Tulsa St, Chatsworth
10637 Andora St, Chatsworth

### Resort
Travelodge, 16117 Ventura Bl, Encino

### Retired Gangster
Back road to Conejo Valley Airport, Thousand Oaks
Janss Ranch/Cameron Center, 288 Greenmeadow Dr, Thousand Oaks

### Revenge (Season 3)
Southern Pacific Chatsworth Train Station, Chatsworth
Cabin Cafe, 20852 Devonshire St, Chatsworth
Intersection, Andora Ave and Faralone Ave, Chatsworth

### Revenge (Season 4)
1344 N Beverly Dr, Beverly Hills
1364 N Beverly Dr, Beverly Hills
1450 N Beverly Dr, Beverly Hills
Upper Franklin Canyon, Beverly Hills
Upper house, Upper Franklin Canyon Reservoir, Beverly Hills

### Reward
Fern Dell, Los Angeles

### Road-Block
Highway 101, Agoura, east of the Palo Comado Canyon Rd bridge
Seminole Hot Springs Inn, 29008 Agoura Rd, Agoura
Golden Pheasant Restaurant/Billingsley Steak House, 26300 Ventura Bl, Calabasas
Highway 101/Ventura Bl and Las Virgenes Rd, Calabasas

### Runaway Boy
7416 Willoughby Ave, Los Angeles
857 N Martel Ave, Los Angeles
903 N Martel Ave, Los Angeles
SW corner Poinsettia Pl and Romaine St, Los Angeles

Forest Lawn Dr, Burbank
ZIV Studio, Los Angeles

## *Safecracker*
Town & Country Cafe, 10255 Topanga Canyon Bl, Chatsworth
Maggi's Italian Kitchen, 21629 Devonshire St, Chatsworth
Verdugo Escrow, 17319 Saticoy St, Van Nuys
Guy's Sporting Goods, 17321 Saticoy St, Van Nuys
Greene Jewelers, 17322 Saticoy St, Van Nuys
Chatsworth Community Church, 10051 Topanga Canyon Bl, Chatsworth
Topanga Canyon Bl north of Church, Chatsworth
10210 Owensmouth Ave, Chatsworth

## *Scared Cop*
possibly near Woodlake Ave and Strathern St, Canoga Park
possibly March Ave and Ingomar St, Canoga Park
Woodlake Ave and Justice St, Canoga Park
1011 N Fuller, Los Angeles
ZIV Studio, Los Angeles

## *The Search*
Cabin Cafe, 20852 Devonshire St, Chatsworth
DeSoto Ave south of Devonshire St, Chatsworth
probably North Hollywood Concrete Tile Co, 12323 Sherman Wy, North Hollywood
Hickory House, 12105 Burbank Bl, North Hollywood
Sego Nursery, 12116 Burbank Bl, North Hollywood

## *The 7th Green*
Knollwood Country Club, 12024 Balboa Bl, Granada Hills

## *Slain Cabby*
Mulholland Dr and Bowmont Dr, Los Angeles
Nifty Food Market, 4742 Woodman Ave, Sherman Oaks
Knoll Crest Realty, 12800 Victory Bl, North Hollywood
House, 12764 Victory Bl, North Hollywood
Nory's Gifts & Jewelry, 13644 Burbank Bl, Sherman Oaks
Wardwell Hardware, 13636 Burbank Bl, Sherman Oaks
Permanent Wave Shop, across street from 13636 Burbank Bl
ZIV Studio, Los Angeles

## *The Sniper*
Upper Franklin Canyon Reservoir, Beverly Hills
Lower house, Upper Franklin Canyon Reservoir, Beverly Hills
Upper house, Upper Franklin Canyon Reservoir, Beverly Hills

## *Split Robbery*
Steele's Motor Lodge, 13949 Ventura Bl, Sherman Oaks
Building, 14060 Ventura Bl, Sherman Oaks
Ralphs, 14049 Ventura Bl, Sherman Oaks

Apartments, 14047 Moorpark St, Sherman Oaks
House, 4242 Goodland Av, Studio City
House, 4320 Goodland Av, Studio City
Goodland Av south of Bloomfield St, Studio City
Between Goodland Av and Valley Spring Ln on Valleyheart Dr, Studio City
Between Alcove Av and Goodland Av on Valleyheart Dr, Studio City
SE corner of Valley Spring Ln and Bellaire Ave, Studio City
Next to Weddington Golf on Valley Spring Ln, Studio City
SE corner of Ventura Bl and Coldwater Canyon Ave, Studio City

### Statute of Limitations
Anita, 18361 Sherman Way, Reseda
McMahan Furniture Store, 18344 Sherman Way, Reseda
CHP Headquarters, behind Magnolia Science Academy, 18238 Sherman Way, Reseda

### Stolen Car Ring
Frank's Nurseries, 12424 Wilshire Bl, Los Angeles
Douglas Park, Wilshire Bl and Chelsea Ave, Los Angeles
1124 Chelsea Ave, Los Angeles
1130 Chelsea Ave, Los Angeles
Mormon Temple, 10777 Santa Monica Bl, Los Angeles
Travelodge, 10740 Santa Monica Bl, Los Angeles
California Bank, 11944 San Vicente Bl, Los Angeles
Alley between 11975 and 11969 San Vicente Bl, Los Angeles
Corner, San Vicente Bl and La Mesa Dr, West Los Angeles
ZIV Studio, Los Angeles

### Stolen Plane-Copter
Whiteman Airport, 12653 Osborne St, Los Angeles
Bronson Canyon, Los Angeles

### Stripped Cars
Barn site approximately where Semrad Rd would cross Bell Creek between Highlander Rd and
    Hartland St, West Hills (Castle Peak in background)

### Suicide
Southern Pacific Glendale Train Station, Glendale
House, 1724 Gardena Av, Glendale
Railroad St, Glendale
Research Craft Plastics Corp, 1011 N Fuller Ave, Los Angeles

### Suspected Cop
Union Oil Service Station, 2000 Hillhurst Ave, Los Angeles
Hillhurst Variety Store, 2068 Hillhurst Ave, Los Angeles
2535 N Vermont Ave, Los Angeles
St. Mary of the Angels Episcopal Church, 4510 Finley Ave, Los Angeles
NW corner Hillhurst Ave and Finley Ave, Los Angeles
North of Greek Theater, N Vermont Ave, Los Angeles

## Taxi

Weddington St and Bakman Ave, Los Angeles
Gas Station, Colfax Ave and Riverside Dr, Los Angeles
6009 Colfax Ave, Los Angeles
6013 Colfax Ave, Los Angeles
6025 Colfax Ave, Los Angeles
corner of Colfax Ave and Oxnard St, Los Angeles
Oxnard St east of Colfax Ave, Los Angeles
Garages at alley next to 11643 Otsego St, Los Angeles
2727 Benedict Canyon Dr, Los Angeles

## Tear Gas Copter

Mountain Patrol Fire Station 2, 16500 Mulholland Dr, Encino
Hilltop house, above intersection of Summitridge Dr and Beverly Park St, Beverly Hills

## Temptation

2025 Nichols Canyon Rd, Los Angeles
Willow Glen Rd and Zorada Dr, Los Angeles
7801 Sunset Bl, Los Angeles
1309 Genessee Ave, Los Angeles
intersection Fountain Ave and Genesee Ave, Los Angeles
Pacific Electric Sherman Yard, 8800 Santa Monica Bl, West Los Angeles
Sunset Tower Hotel, 9358 Sunset Bl, West Los Angeles

## Trailer Story

Verdugo Escrow, 17319 Saticoy St, Van Nuys
Guy's Sporting Goods, 17321 Saticoy St, Van Nuys
Greene Jewelers and Gift Wear, 17322 Saticoy St, Van Nuys
Street, 12800 Victory Bl, Los Angeles
The Norman Larson Company, Van Nuys Airport, Van Nuys

## Train Copter

8627 Reseda Bl, Northridge
8727 Reseda Bl, Northridge
8725 Reseda Bl, Northridge
18333 Eddy St, Northridge
Northridge Train Station, Northridge

## Train Robbery

Simi Valley Train Station, across street from 4563 Los Angeles Ave, Simi Valley
Towing Garage, 4456 Los Angeles Ave, Simi Valley

## Transmitter Danger

Palmer's Market, 7714 Fountain Ave, Los Angeles
Apartments, 7733 Hampton Ave, Los Angeles
Apartments, 7719 Hampton Ave, Los Angeles

## The Trap

Merrill's Feed & Saddlery, 22705 Ventura Bl, Woodland Hills

William R. Wilson, Jr., Insurance, 22708 Ventura Bl, Woodland Hills
Lee's Steak House, Hideaway Room, 22611 Ventura Bl, Woodland Hills
Neider's Body Shop, 22440 Ventura Blvd, Woodland Hills
Ventura Bl east of 101 freeway exit, Woodland Hills
Sale Ave and Del Valle St, Woodland Hills
House on SW corner Avenue San Luis and Fallbrook Ave, Woodland Hills
Avenue San Luis and Shoup Ave, Woodland Hills
Woodland Hills Pet Shop, 22543 Ventura Bl, Woodland Hills

*Trojan Horse*
Mulholland Dr and Bowmont Dr, Los Angeles
House nearest Mulholland Dr, Bowmont Dr, Los Angeles
ZIV Studio, Los Angeles

*The Trucker*
Griffith Park Fern Dell Nature Museum, 5375 Red Oak Dr, Los Angeles
Cafe (now The Trails), 2333 Fern Dell Dr, Los Angeles
Coffee Shop, in Griffith Park Center, Los Angeles
ZIV Studio, Los Angeles

*Typhoid Carrier*
The Wooden Shoe Cafe, 8240 Topanga Canyon Bl, Canoga Park
Curragh Stock Farm, 22901 Roscoe Bl (nw of Fallbrook Ave and Eccles St), Canoga Park
CHP Headquarters, 936 Poinsettia Pl, Los Angeles
ZIV Studio, Los Angeles

*Witness Wife*
Mountain Patrol Fire Station 2, 16500 Mulholland Dr, Encino
Hilltop house, above intersection of Summitridge Dr and Beverly Park St, Beverly Hills

*Woman Escapes*
Joe Ole's Hardware, 4543 Van Nuys Bl, Encino
Erma May Robbins Cosmetics, 4531 Van Nuys Bl, Encino
Sherman Oaks Vacuums, 4529 Van Nuys Bl, Encino
Mountain Patrol Fire Station 2, 16500 Mulholland Dr, Encino

*Wounded*
2239 Canyon Dr, Los Angeles
2606 Canyon Dr, Los Angeles

# LOCATION GUIDE

## LOS ANGELES COUNTY

| | | | |
|---|---|---|---|
| Chavez Ravine | | | Los Angeles |
| **Bank Messenger** | | | |
| **Confidence Game** | | | |
| **Credit Card** | | | |
| **Dan Hostage** | | | |
| **Dead Hunter** | | | |
| **Deaf Mute** | | | |
| **Family Affair** | | | |
| **Fear** | | | |
| **Hostage Officer** | | | |
| **Illegal Entry** | | | |
| **Lady Bandits** | | | |
| House | | Davis St | Los Angeles |
| **Family Affair** | | | |
| **Hostage Officer** | | | |
| Intersection | | Davis St and Giraldi St | Los Angeles |
| **Hostage Officer** | | | |
| De Leon City Center Grocery Store | 1146 | Effie St | Los Angeles |
| **Confidence Game** | | | |
| **Dead Hunter** | | | |
| **Deaf Mute** | | | |
| **Hideout** | | | |
| De Leon House | 1151 | Effie St | Los Angeles |
| **Confidence Game** | | | |
| **Dan Hostage** | | | |
| **Deaf Mute** | | | |
| **Hideout** | | | |
| Palo Verde Elementary School | 1029 | Effie St | Los Angeles |
| **Confidence Game** | | | |
| Intersection and House | | Chavez Ravine Rd and Boylston St | Los Angeles |
| **Lady Bandits** | | | |
| Road west of 110 Freeway | | Lilac Terrace | Los Angeles |
| **Hitch Hiker** | | | |

| | | | |
|---|---|---|---|
| Traveling shot | W | 1st St and Arden Bl | Los Angeles |
| **Chain Store** | | | |
| Traveling shot | | 1st and Lucerne | Los Angeles |
| **Chain Store** | | | |
| House | 701 E | 222nd St | Carson |
| **Auto Press** | | | |
| Elysian Park Adaptive Recreation Center | 835 | Academy Rd | Los Angeles |
| **Hitch Hiker** | | | |
| **Illegal Entry** | | | |
| Los Angeles Police Academy | 1880 | Academy Rd | Los Angeles |
| **Hideout** | | | |
| Restaurant, Gas Station | 29001 | Agoura Rd | Agoura Hills |
| **Desert Town** | | | |
| **Frightened Witness** | | | |
| **Phony Insurance** | | | |
| **Prisoner Exchange Copter** | | | |

| | | | |
|---|---|---|---|
| Seminole Hot Springs Inn | 29008 | Agoura Rd | Agoura Hills |
| **Frightened Witness** | | | |
| **Human Bomb** | | | |
| **Phony Insurance** | | | |
| **Road-Block** | | | |
| **Prisoner Exchange Copter** | | | |
| Agoura Stock Farm | | Agoura Rd west of Cornell Rd | Agoura Hills |
| **Frightened Witness** | | | |
| **Prisoner Exchange Copter** | | | |
| Joe Tommaso Market | 1041 | Alpine St | Los Angeles |
| **Lady Bandits** | | | |
| House | 1117 | Alpine St | Los Angeles |
| **False Confession** | | | |
| Alley west of | 1119-1117 | Alpine St | Los Angeles |
| **False Confession** | | | |
| Apartments | | Alpine St and White Knoll Dr | Los Angeles |
| **False Confession** | | | |
| Alley off | | Alpine St between Beaudry Av and White Knoll Dr | Los Angeles |
| **False Confession** | | | |
| Harry E. McConnell Service Station | 1000 N | Alvarado St | Los Angeles |
| **Credit Card** | | | |
| House | 3660 | Amesbury Rd | Los Angeles |
| **Double Death** | | | |
| House | 10637 | Andora Av | Chatsworth |
| **Resident Officer** | | | |
| Intersection | | Andora Av and Faralone Av | Chatsworth |
| **Revenge** (Season 3) | | | |
| Bank | 15301 | Antioch St | Pacific Palisades |
| **Harbor Story** | | | |
| Building | 15322 | Antioch St | Pacific Palisades |
| **Harbor Story** | | | |
| Hardware | 15328 | Antioch St | Pacific Palisades |
| **Harbor Story** | | | |
| alley between | 15317 | Antioch St and 910 Via De La Paz | Pacific Palisades |
| **Harbor Story** | | | |
| House on SW corner | 22800 | Avenue San Luis and Fallbrook Av | Woodland Hills |
| **The Trap** | | | |
| Intersection | 22321 | Avenue San Luis and Shoup Ave | Woodland Hills |
| **The Trap** | | | |
| Building | 5150 | Babcock Av | Valley Village |
| **Phony Cop** | | | |
| Spudnutt Shop | 10705 | Balboa Bl | Granada Hills |
| **Female Hitchhiker** | | | |
| Houses | 10718 to 10732 | Balboa Bl | Granada Hills |
| **Female Hitchhiker** | | | |
| Apartments | 10727 | Balboa Bl | Granada Hills |
| **Female Hitchhiker** | | | |
| Jebs Restaurant | 7600 | Balboa Bl | Van Nuys |
| **Hot Rod** | | | |
| Perrygraf Slide-Chart | 150 S | Barrington Av | Los Angeles |
| **Christmas Story** | | | |

| Location | Number | Street | City |
|---|---|---|---|
| House | 2330 N | Beachwood Dr | Los Angeles |
| **Art Robbery** | | | |
| Bernadine Apartments | 2400 N | Beachwood Dr | Los Angeles |
| **Art Robbery** | | | |
| House | 2420 N | Beachwood Dr | Los Angeles |
| **Art Robbery** | | | |
| Apartments | 2438 N | Beachwood Dr | Los Angeles |
| **Art Robbery** | | | |
| Alley exit between | 2673 and 2677 N | Beachwood Dr | Los Angeles |
| **Mother's March** | | | |
| Alley on side of | 2691 N | Beachwood Dr | Los Angeles |
| **Mother's March** | | | |
| Hill-Top Beauty Salon | 2691 N | Beachwood Dr | Los Angeles |
| **Mother's March** | | | |
| Jim Woolvin Richfield Gas Station | 2694 N | Beachwood Dr | Los Angeles |
| **Blast Area-Copter** | | | |
| House | 2800 N | Beachwood Dr | Los Angeles |
| **Mother's March** | | | |
| House | 2837 N | Beachwood Dr | Los Angeles |
| **Mother's March** | | | |
| House | 2838 N | Beachwood Dr | Los Angeles |
| **Mother's March** | | | |
| House | 3074 N | Beachwood Dr | Los Angeles |
| **Rabies** | | | |
| Traveling shot | towards Glen Oak | Beachwood Dr | Los Angeles |
| **Mother's March** | | | |
| Traveling shot | S | Beachwood Dr and W 2nd St | Los Angeles |
| **Chain Store** | | | |
| Driveway between | 496 and 498 N | Beaudry Av | Los Angeles |
| **False Confession** | | | |
| Traveling shot | N | Beaudry Av near Figueroa Terrace | Los Angeles |
| **False Confession** | | | |
| Texaco Service Station | 2707 | Belden Dr | Los Angeles |
| **Rabies** | | | |
| House | 2727 | Benedict Canyon Dr | Los Angeles |
| **Kidnap-Copter** | | | |
| **Taxi** | | | |
| House | 1344 N | Beverly Dr | Beverly Hills |
| **Revenge** (Season 4) | | | |
| House | 1364 N | Beverly Dr | Beverly Hills |
| **Revenge** (Season 4) | | | |
| House | 1450 N | Beverly Dr | Beverly Hills |
| **Revenge** (Season 4) | | | |
| Apartments | 1643 S | Beverly Glen Bl | Los Angeles |
| **Portrait of Death** | | | |
| Four Oaks Restaurant | 2181 N | Beverly Glen Bl | Los Angeles |
| **Careless Cop** | | | |
| **Portrait of Death** | | | |
| San Fernando Jr High Auditorium | 130 N | Brand Bl | San Fernando |
| **Escort** | | | |
| Hotel Goodhap | 208 S | Brand Bl | San Fernando |
| **Machine-Napping** | | | |
| Ross Cleaners | 1708 N | Bronson Av | Los Angeles |
| **Missing Witness** | | | |
| Hickory House | 12105 | Burbank Bl | Valley Village |

| Location | Number | Street | City |
|---|---|---|---|
| **The Search** | | | |
| Sego Nursery | 12116 | Burbank Bl | Valley Village |
| **The Search** | | | |
| Wardwell Hardware | 13636 | Burbank Bl | Sherman Oaks |
| **Slain Cabby** | | | |
| Permanent Wave Shop, across street from | 13636 | Burbank Bl | Sherman Oaks |
| **Slain Cabby** | | | |
| Nory's Gifts & Jewelry | 13644 | Burbank Bl | Sherman Oaks |
| **Slain Cabby** | | | |
| just west of Sperling Nursery | | Calabasas Rd | Calabasas |
| **Gambling** | | | |
| east of Mureau Rd | | Calabasas Rd | Calabasas |
| **Gambling** | | | |
| Intersection looking east | west int, not east | Calatrana Dr and Medina Rd | Woodland Hills |
| **Released Convict** | | | |
| House and garage | NE corner of | Campo Rd and Providencia St | Woodland Hills |
| **Released Convict** | | | |
| Bronson Canyon | | Canyon Dr | Los Angeles |
| **Art Robbery** | | | |
| **Blast Area-Copter** | | | |
| **Cargo Hi Jack** | | | |
| **Copter Cave In** | | | |
| **Human Bomb** | | | |
| **Insulin** | | | |
| **Missing Witness** | | | |
| **Prisoner Exchange Copter** | | | |
| **Prospector** | | | |
| **Stolen Plane-Copter** | | | |
| Bronson Canyon Entrance | | Canyon Dr | Los Angeles |
| **Missing Witness** | | | |
| House | 2239 | Canyon Dr | Los Angeles |
| **Wounded** | | | |
| House | 2243 | Canyon Dr | Los Angeles |
| **Officer's Wife** | | | |
| House | 2245 | Canyon Dr | Los Angeles |
| **Insulin** | | | |
| House | 2606 | Canyon Dr | Los Angeles |
| **Wounded** | | | |
| House | 2633 | Canyon Dr | Los Angeles |
| **The Collector** | | | |
| corner | | Canyon Dr and Bronson Hill Dr | Los Angeles |
| **Insulin** | | | |
| House | 2707 | Canyon Dr | Los Angeles |
| **Missing Witness** | | | |
| Alley between | | Canyon Dr to Bronson Av to Carlton Wy to Harold Wy | Los Angeles |
| **The Collector** | | | |
| Safeway Market | 1212 | Celis St | San Fernando |
| **Machine-Napping** | | | |
| Building | | Celis St and Brand Bl | San Fernando |
| **Machine-Napping** | | | |
| Traveling shot | 800 block | Centennial St | Los Angeles |
| **Bank Messenger** | | | |
| D. N. Nicassio Real Estate | 802 | Centennial St | Los Angeles |

**Confidence Game**
**Lady Bandits**

| | | | |
|---|---|---|---|
| corner | | Centennial St and Alpine St | Los Angeles |

**Lady Bandits**

| | | | |
|---|---|---|---|
| Intersection | NE Corner of | Centennial St and New Depot | Los Angeles |

**Bank Messenger**

| | | | |
|---|---|---|---|
| Central Motel | 1516 S | Central Av | Glendale |

**Express Delivery**

| | | | |
|---|---|---|---|
| House | 1681 S | Central Av | Glendale |

**Hostage**

| | | | |
|---|---|---|---|
| Traveling shot | | Cerritos Av | Glendale |

**Express Delivery**

| | | | |
|---|---|---|---|
| SP Glendale Train Station | 400 W | Cerritos Av | Glendale |

**Express Delivery**
**Framed Cop**
**Gem Robbery** (Season 2)
**Gem Robbery** (Season 4)
**Hostage**
**Suicide**

| | | | |
|---|---|---|---|
| Intersection | | Cerritos Av and Gardena Av | Glendale |

**Hostage**

| | | | |
|---|---|---|---|
| West of T.C. Blvd | | Chatsworth St | Chatsworth |
| Apartments | 1124 | Chelsea Av | Los Angeles |

**Stolen Car Ring**

| | | | |
|---|---|---|---|
| Apartments | 1130 | Chelsea Av | Los Angeles |

**Stolen Car Ring**

| | | | |
|---|---|---|---|
| DeLongpre Park | 1350 N | Cherokee Av | Los Angeles |

**Killer on the Run**

| | | | |
|---|---|---|---|
| Chancellor Apartments | 1842 N | Cherokee Av | Los Angeles |

**Released Convict**

| | | | |
|---|---|---|---|
| Traveling shot | South of 34278 around the curve | Cheseboro Rd | Palmdale |

**Desert-Copter**

| | | | |
|---|---|---|---|
| Traveling shot | | Cheseboro Rd and Mt Emma Rd | Palmdale |

**Desert-Copter**

| | | | |
|---|---|---|---|
| Building | 915 N | Citrus Av | Los Angeles |

**Girl Bandit**

| | | | |
|---|---|---|---|
| Stationary shot | along PCH | Civic Center Wy | Malibu |

**Harbor Story**

| | | | |
|---|---|---|---|
| Traveling shot | | Civic Center Wy and Malibu Canyon Rd | Malibu |

**Harbor Story**

| | | | |
|---|---|---|---|
| Traveling Shot south side between Kenwood St and Screenland Dr | | Clark Av | Burbank |

**License Plates**

| | | | |
|---|---|---|---|
| Jerry McGurrin Realtor | 3711 | Clark Av | Burbank |

**License Plates**

| | | | |
|---|---|---|---|
| Colfax Cleaners | 4360 | Coldwater Canyon Av | Los Angeles |

**Deadly Diamonds**

| | | | |
|---|---|---|---|
| House | 5470 | Coldwater Canyon Av | Valley Village |

**Phony Cop**

| | | | |
|---|---|---|---|
| House | 5439 | Coldwater Canyon Av | Sherman Oaks |

**Phony Cop**

| | | | |
|---|---|---|---|
| House | 6009 | Colfax Av | Los Angeles |

**Taxi**

| | | | |
|---|---|---|---|
| House | 6013 | Colfax Av | Los Angeles |
| **Taxi** | | | |
| Intersection | corner of | Colfax Av and Oxnard St | Los Angeles |
| **Taxi** | | | |
| Gas Station | SW corner | Colfax Av and Riverside Dr | Los Angeles |
| **Taxi** | | | |
| Traveling shot looking north from 2121 | | Commonwealth Av | Los Angeles |
| **Double Death** | | | |
| Apartment | 2105 N | Commonwealth Av | Los Angeles |
| **Double Death** | | | |
| Houe | 2115 N | Commonwealth Av | Los Angeles |
| **Double Death** | | | |
| Apartment | 2121 N | Commonwealth Av | Los Angeles |
| **Double Death** | | | |
| Intersection | | Comstock and Holman | Los Angeles |
| **Portrait of Death** | | | |
| Traveling shot | | Comstock Av north from Santa Monica Bl | Los Angeles |
| **Portrait of Death** | | | |
| Traveling shot | | Courtney Av and Hollywood Blvd | Los Angeles |
| **Brave Boy** | | | |
| Bridge over Ballona Creek eastward | | Culver Bl | Playa Del Rey |
| **Reckless Driving** | | | |
| East of Lincoln Bl | | Culver Bl | Playa Del Rey |
| **Reckless Driving** | | | |
| Apartments | 12755 | Culver Bl | Los Angeles |
| **Hit and Run** (Season 1) | | | |
| Building | 185 | Culver Bl | Playa Del Rey |
| **Radioactive** | | | |
| Building | 200 | Culver Bl | Playa Del Rey |
| **Radioactive** | | | |
| Apartments | 1120 N | Curson Av | Los Angeles |
| **Brave Boy** | | | |
| Grand Central Warehouse | 7115 | Darby Av | Reseda |
| **Phony Insurance** | | | |
| Dr. R. L. Snow | 7125 | Darby Av | Reseda |
| **Phony Insurance** | | | |
| Building | 7131 | Darby Av | Reseda |
| **Phony Insurance** | | | |
| Building, SW corner | | Darby Av and Gault St | Reseda |
| **Phony Insurance** | | | |
| Street towards north | 9644 | DeSoto Av | Chatsworth |
| **Narcotics** | | | |
| Street w/house in background | | DeSoto Av above Rinaldi | Chatsworth |
| **Narcotics** | | | |
| Street view | | DeSoto Av south of Devonshire St | Chatsworth |
| **The Search** | | | |
| Cabin Cafe | 20852 | Devonshire St | Chatsworth |
| **Hired Killer** | | | |
| **Narcotics** | | | |
| **Revenge** (Season 3) | | | |
| **The Search** | | | |
| Shopping Cart | 21360 | Devonshire St | Chatsworth |
| **Fake Cop** | | | |

| | | | |
|---|---|---|---|
| Maggi's Italian Kitchen | 21629 | Devonshire St | Chatsworth |
| **Safecracker** | | | |
| Building | 21743 | Devonshire St | Chatsworth |
| **Hitchhiker** | | | |
| Elizabeth's Cafe | 21754 | Devonshire St | Chatsworth |
| **Hired Killer** | | | |
| Greene Jewelers across street from | 21757 | Devonshire St | Chatsworth |
| **Hitchhiker** | | | |
| Building | 21800 | Devonshire St | Chatsworth |
| **Hitchhiker** | | | |
| Chatsworth Cleaners | 21824 | Devonshire St | Chatsworth |
| **Fake Cop** | | | |
| House and intersection | | Devonshire St and Andora | Chatsworth |
| **Fake Cop** | | | |
| House | 3700 | Dover St | Glendale |
| **Hostage** | | | |
| House | 3704 | Dover St | Glendale |
| **Hostage** | | | |
| Intersection | | Dover St and Brunswick Av | Glendale |
| **Hostage** | | | |
| Street looking west towards curve | east of Villena Av | Dumetz Rd | Woodland Hills |
| **Released Convict** | | | |
| intersection | at Serrania Av | Dumetz Rd | Woodland Hills |
| **Gambling** | | | |
| intersection looking east and house ast side of int | | Dumetz Rd and Campo Rd | Woodland Hills |
| **Released Convict** | | | |
| SP Chatsworth Train Station | east of corner of | Dupont St and Remmet Av | Chatsworth |
| **Hired Killer** | | | |
| **Revenge** (Season 3) | | | |
| House | 10374 | Eastborne Av | Los Angeles |
| **Portrait of Death** | | | |
| Apartments | 10403 | Eastborne Av | Los Angeles |
| **Portrait of Death** | | | |
| Apartments | 10407 | Eastborne Av | Los Angeles |
| **Portrait of Death** | | | |
| Building | 18333 | Eddy St | Northridge |
| **Train Copter** | | | |
| Seers Lumber | 356 | El Segundo Bl | Hawthorne |
| **Car Theft** | | | |
| Frosty's Towing | 3924 W | El Segundo Bl | Hawthorne |
| **Car Theft** | | | |
| Building | 3940 W | El Segundo Bl | Hawthorne |
| **Car Theft** | | | |
| Buildings on SE corner | | El Segundo Bl and Roselle Av | Hawthorne |
| **Car Theft** | | | |
| House | 5713 | Eveward Rd | Culver City |
| **Radioactive** | | | |

## EXPOSITION PARK

| | | | |
|---|---|---|---|
| Dr Theodor T Alexander Jr Science Center | 3980 | Bill Robertson Ln | Los Angeles |
| **Desperate Men** | | | |
| Exposition Park | 3980 | Bill Robertson Ln | Los Angeles |
| **Desperate Men** | | | |

| | | | |
|---|---|---|---|
| Cabin | near north end | Farralone Av | |
| **Female Hitchhiker** | | | |
| Rear of house | 10346 | Farralone Av | Chatsworth |
| **Fake Cop** | | | |
| Peterson Dairy Farm | 9409 | Farralone Av | Chatsworth |
| **Mental Patient** | | | |
| Cafe (now The Trails) | 2333 | Fern Dell Dr | Los Angeles |
| **Rabies** | | | |
| **The Trucker** | | | |
| Fern Dell | | | Los Angeles |
| **Hot Dust** | | | |
| **Policewoman** | | | |
| Fern Dell | | | Los Angeles |
| **Gem Robbery** (Season 2) | | | |
| **Policewoman** | | | |
| **Reward** | | | |
| Building | 871 | Figueroa Terrace | Los Angeles |
| **False Confession** | | | |
| Traveling shot | | Figueroa Terrace and Pasadena Fwy Exit | Los Angeles |
| **False Confession** | | | |
| Traveling shot | | Figueroa Terrace and W College St | Los Angeles |
| **False Confession** | | | |
| Apartments | 4452 | Finley Av | Los Angeles |
| **Reformation** | | | |
| St. Mary of the Angels Episcopal Church | 4510 | Finley Av | Los Angeles |
| **Reformation** | | | |
| **Suspected Cop** | | | |
| Traveling shot | | Foothill Bl near Balboa Bl | Los Angeles |
| **Escort** | | | |
| Traveling shot | | Foothill Bl near Filbert St | Los Angeles |
| **Escort** | | | |
| House corner | | Foothill Dr and Bronson Av | Los Angeles |
| **The Collector** | | | |
| Apartment corner | | Foothill Dr and Canyon Dr | Los Angeles |
| **The Collector** | | | |
| Travling shot | | Forest Lawn Dr | Burbank |
| **Hitchhiker Dies** | | | |
| **Runaway Boy** | | | |
| Ad-Type | 916 N | Formosa Av | Los Angeles |
| **Hot Cargo** | | | |
| Building | 922 N | Formosa Av | Los Angeles |
| **Hot Cargo** | | | |
| Apartment | 941 N | Formosa Av | Los Angeles |
| **Hot Cargo** | | | |
| Storage Tank on Formosa near Santa Monica Bl | across street from United Artists Studio | Formosa Av | Los Angeles |
| **Human Bomb** | | | |
| Building | SE corner | Formosa Av and Romaine St | Los Angeles |
| **Hot Cargo** | | | |

486

| Location | Number | Street | City |
|---|---|---|---|
| Building | NE corner | Formosa Av and Willoughby Av | Los Angeles |
| **Hot Cargo** | | | |
| Apartments | NW corner | Formosa Av and Willoughby Av | Los Angeles |
| **Hot Cargo** | | | |
| Former Cedars of Lebanon Hospital (now Scientology) | 4833 | Fountain Av | Los Angeles |
| **Blood Money** | | | |
| Palmer's Market | 7714 | Fountain Av | Los Angeles |
| **Transmitter Danger** | | | |
| intersection from north side | | Fountain Av and Genesee Av | Los Angeles |
| **Temptation** | | | |
| Bronsonia Pharmacy | 5889 | Franklin Av | Los Angeles |
| **The Collector** | | | |
| Upper Franklin Canyon Reservoir | | Franklin Canyon Reservoir | Beverly Hills |
| **Breath of a Child** | | | |
| **Escaped Mental Patient** | | | |
| **Fisherman's Luck** | | | |
| **Psycho-Killer** | | | |
| **Revenge** (Season 4) | | | |
| **The Sniper** | | | |
| Lower house | Upper | Franklin Canyon Reservoir | Beverly Hills |
| **Breath of a Child** | | | |
| **Escaped Mental Patient** | | | |
| **Fisherman's Luck** | | | |
| **Psycho-Killer** | | | |
| **The Sniper** | | | |
| Upper house | Upper | Franklin Canyon Reservoir | Beverly Hills |
| **Breath of a Child** | | | |
| **Psycho-Killer** | | | |
| **Revenge** (Season 4) | | | |
| **The Sniper** | | | |
| Lower Franklin Canyon Reservoir | | Lake Dr | Beverly Hills |
| **Psycho** | | | |
| Traveling shot | | Franklin Canyon Dr and Beverly Pl | Los Angeles |
| **Escaped Mental Patient** | | | |
| Research Craft Plastics Corp | 1011 N | Fuller Av | Los Angeles |
| **Prospector** | | | |
| **Scared Cop** | | | |
| **Suicide** | | | |
| ZIV Studio exterior | N | Fuller Av | Los Angeles |
| **Careless Cop** | | | |
| **Girl Bandit** | | | |
| ZIV Studio exterior | South on | Fuller Av to Romaine St | Los Angeles |
| **Hitchhiker Dies** | | | |
| House | 4459 | Gainsborough Av | Los Angeles |
| **Dead Hunter** | | | |
| House | 1724 | Gardena Av | Glendale |
| **Suicide** | | | |
| House | 1729 | Gardena Av | Glendale |
| **Express Delivery** | | | |

**Gem Robbery** (Season 4)

| | | | |
|---|---|---|---|
| House | 1309 | Genesee Av | Los Angeles |
| **Temptation** | | | |
| House | 1609 N | Genesee Av | Los Angeles |
| **Explosives** | | | |
| House | 728 | Genesee Av | Los Angeles |
| **Gambling Story** | | | |
| Houses odd side next to alley | 721 | Genesee Ave | Los Angeles |
| **Gambling Story** | | | |
| House | 715 | Genesee Ave | Los Angeles |
| **Gambling Story** | | | |
| Safeway Market | 3080 | Glendale Bl | Los Angeles |
| **Hostage** | | | |
| Club Tee Yee | 3208 | Glendale Bl | Los Angeles |
| **Hostage** | | | |
| Building | 3210 | Glendale Bl | Los Angeles |
| **Hostage** | | | |
| Building | 3212 | Glendale Bl | Los Angeles |
| **Hostage** | | | |
| Street south of Bloomfield St | | Goodland Av | Studio City |
| **Split Robbery** | | | |
| House | 4242 | Goodland Av | Studio City |
| **Split Robbery** | | | |
| House | 1233 | Greenacre Av | Los Angeles |
| **Hitchhiker Dies** | | | |
| Church Building at alley between Reseda Bl and Baird Av | | Gresham St | Northridge |
| **Confession** | | | |

## GRIFFITH PARK

| | | | |
|---|---|---|---|
| Griffith Park Boy's Camp Entrance Area | 4730 | Crystal Springs Dr | Los Angeles |
| **Rabies** | | | |
| Griffith Park Boy's Camp | 4730 | Crystal Springs Dr | Los Angeles |
| **Amnesia** | | | |
| **Dan's Vacation** | | | |
| **Mountain-Copter** | | | |
| **Rabies** | | | |
| **Reformation** | | | |
| Griffith Park | | | |
| **Convicted Innocent** | | | |
| **Convict's Wife** | | | |
| **Reformation** | | | |
| Griffith Park Collidge Golf Course | | Crystal Springs Rd | Los Angeles |
| **Convict's Wife** | | | |
| Griffith Park near Golf Academy Entrance | | Crystal Springs Rd | Los Angeles |
| **Cargo Hi Jack** | | | |
| Griffith Park Pony Ride | | Crystal Springs Rd | Los Angeles |
| **Convict's Wife** | | | |
| Coffee Shop | | Griffith Park Center | Los Angeles |
| **Convict's Wife** | | | |
| **The Trucker** | | | |

| | | | |
|---|---|---|---|
| Apartments | 7719 | Hampton Av | Los Angeles |
| **Transmitter Danger** | | | |
| Apartments | 7733 | Hampton Av | Los Angeles |
| **Transmitter Danger** | | | |
| Shotout scee | 2615 | Harlesden Ct | Los Angeles |
| **Killer on the Run** | | | |
| Restaurant | 15603 | Hawthorne Bl | Lawndale |

| | | | |
|---|---|---|---|
| **Lookout** | | | |
| NE corner, Willoughby side | 900 | Highland Av | West L.A. |
| **Girl Bandit** | | | |
| NW corner, Willoughby side | 901 | Highland Av | West L.A. |
| **Girl Bandit** | | | |
| Opening Credits Exit | | Highway 101 east of the Palo Comado Canyon Rd bridge | Agoura |
| **Road-Block** | | | |
| Traveling shot | | Highway 101 east of Mureau Rd | Calabasas |
| **Gambling** | | | |
| House | 854 | Hillcrest St | El Segundo |
| **Lookout** | | | |
| Sports Field | | Hillcrest St and Walnut Av | El Segundo |
| **Lookout** | | | |
| CHP Headquarters | 1662 | Hillhurst Av | Los Angeles |
| **Double Death** | | | |
| Dept of Water and Power Distributing Station | 1675 | Hillhurst Av | Los Angeles |
| **Dead Hunter** | | | |
| **Double Death** | | | |
| Apartment | 1701 | Hillhurst Av | Los Angeles |
| **Dead Hunter** | | | |
| House, now parking lot | 1714 | Hillhurst Av | Los Angeles |
| **Reformation** | | | |
| Apartment | 1720 | Hillhurst Av | Los Angeles |
| **Dead Hunter** | | | |
| **Reformation** | | | |
| Brownie Letter Shop (City Bank) | 1751 | Hillhurst Av | Los Angeles |
| **Bank Messenger** | | | |
| Ise's Automotive Service | 1774 | Hillhurst Av | Los Angeles |
| **Double Death** | | | |
| Apartments | 1822 | Hillhurst Av | Los Angeles |
| **Double Death** | | | |
| E. D. Cristman Real Estate | 1863 | Hillhurst Av | Los Angeles |
| **Double Death** | | | |
| Union Oil Service Station | 2000 | Hillhurst Av | Los Angeles |
| **Reformation** | | | |
| **Suspected Cop** | | | |
| Hillhurst Mart | 2060 | Hillhurst Av | Los Angeles |
| **Double Death** | | | |
| **Framed Cop** | | | |
| Hillhurst Variety Store | 2068 | Hillhurst Av | Los Angeles |
| **Suspected Cop** | | | |
| Buildings | East side background | Hillhurst Av and Finley Av | Los Angeles |
| **Framed Cop** | | | |
| Building | NW corner | Hillhurst Av and Finley Av | Los Angeles |
| **Reformation** | | | |
| **Suspected Cop** | | | |
| Apartments | SE corner | Hillhurst Av and Kingswell Av | Los Angeles |
| **Dead Hunter** | | | |
| Buildings | East side of intersection | Hillhurst Av and Price St | Los Angeles |
| **Double Death** | | | |

| Location | Number | Street | City |
|---|---|---|---|
| **Framed Cop** | | | |
| House | 10320 | Hillview Av | Chatsworth |
| **Hitchhiker** | | | |
| Colt Ventilation of America Inc. | 4652 | Hollywood Bl | Los Angeles |
| **Hypo Bandit** | | | |
| W. O. Renman Electrical Contractor | 4655 | Hollywood Bl | Los Angeles |
| **Hypo Bandit** | | | |
| Richfield Service Station | 4696 | Hollywood Bl | Los Angeles |
| **Hypo Bandit** | | | |
| Kirk's Drug Store | 817 N | Hollywood Wy | Burbank |
| **License Plates** | | | |
| Furniture Store | 907 N | Hollywood Wy | Burbank |
| **License Plates** | | | |
| Apartment | 1812 | Holmby Av | Los Angeles |
| **Portrait of Death** | | | |
| north side of Woodland Hills Golf Course | | Ibanez Av | Woodland Hills |
| **Gambling** | | | |
| Flight View Restaurant | 310 E | Imperial Av | El Segundo |
| **Reckless Driving** | | | |
| near Flight View Restaurant | 310 E | Imperial Av | El Segundo |
| **Lookout** | | | |
| Buildings | 600 block W | Imperial Av | El Segundo |
| **Lookout** | | | |
| Apartments SE corner | 548 W | Imperial Av and Loma Vista St | El Segundo |
| **Lookout** | | | |
| Traveling shot | | Imperial Hwy next to LAX | Inglewood |
| **Reckless Driving** | | | |
| Baldwin Hills Oil Field | | Jefferson Bl | Culver City |
| **Oil Lease** | | | |
| California Auto Parts & Wrecking Co | 9405 | Jefferson Bl | Culver City |
| **Radioactive** | | | |
| Business | 9425 | Jefferson Bl | Culver City |
| **Radioactive** | | | |
| Business | 9450 | Jefferson Bl | Culver City |
| **Radioactive** | | | |
| Apartments | 1340 | June St | Los Angeles |
| **Killer on the Run** | | | |
| Apartments | 4444-4450 | Kingswell Av | Los Angeles |
| **Reformation** | | | |
| Apartments | 4451 | Kingswell Av | Los Angeles |
| **Reformation** | | | |
| Knollwood Country Club | 12024 | Balboa Bl | Granada Hills |
| **The 7th Green** | | | |
| Danny's Used Cars | 501 N | La Brea Av | Los Angeles |
| **Dead Patrolman** | | | |
| Apartments | 4439 | Lakeside Dr | Burbank |
| **Hitchhiker Dies** | | | |
| W. H. Wilshire Studios | 103 N | Larchmont Bl | Los Angeles |
| **Counterfeit** | | | |
| Businesses | 130 block of N | Larchmont Bl | Los Angeles |
| **Counterfeit** | | | |
| Harper Method Approved Shop | 143 N | Larchmont Bl | Los Angeles |
| **Counterfeit** | | | |
| Landis Department Store | 157 N | Larchmont Bl | Los Angeles |
| **Counterfeit** | | | |
| McCarthy Gift Shop | 161 N | Larchmont Bl | Los Angeles |

| Location | Number | Street | City |
|---|---|---|---|
| **Counterfeit** | | | |
| Behind Wilshire Food Center | 214 N | Larchmont Bl | Los Angeles |
| **Chain Store** | | | |
| Wilshire Food Center | 214 N | Larchmont Bl | Los Angeles |
| **Chain Store** | | | |
| Larchmont Travel Agency | 221 | Larchmont Bl | Los Angeles |
| **Chain Store** | | | |
| Earl Hays Press | 1121 | Las Palmas Av | Los Angeles |
| **Counterfeit** | | | |
| Las Palmas Hotel | 1738 N | Las Palmas Av | Los Angeles |
| **Released Convict** | | | |
| Apartment | 1749 N | Las Palmas Av | Los Angeles |
| **Released Convict** | | | |
| Telephone booth SE corner | N | Las Palmas Av and Yucca St | Los Angeles |
| **Released Convict** | | | |
| Apartment | NE corner N | Las Palmas Av and Yucca St | Los Angeles |
| **Released Convict** | | | |
| House | 4457 | Lexington Av | Los Angeles |
| **Convicted Innocent** | | | |
| House | 4455 | Lexington Av | Los Angeles |
| **Convicted Innocent** | | | |
| House | 4453 | Lexington Av | Los Angeles |
| **Convicted Innocent** | | | |
| House | 1226 | Lilac Pl | Los Angeles |
| **Foster Child** | | | |
| **The Judge** | | | |
| House | 1232 | Lilac Pl | Los Angeles |
| **Foster Child** | | | |
| House | 1233 | Lilac Pl | Los Angeles |
| **The Judge** | | | |
| Apartment next door on right to | 1233 | Lilac Pl | Los Angeles |
| **The Judge** | | | |
| Naval and Marine Corps Reserve Center in background at 1700 Stadium Wy | | Lilac Terrace | Los Angeles |
| **Hitch Hiker** | | | |
| **The Judge** | | | |
| House | 3655 | Longridge Av | Sherman Oaks |
| **Expose** | | | |
| House | 3755 | Longridge Av | Sherman Oaks |
| **Expose** | | | |
| Tracking shot | NW corner of | Longridge Av and Ethel Av | Sherman Oaks |
| **Expose** | | | |
| Tam O'Shanter Inn | 2980 | Los Feliz Bl | Los Angeles |
| **Framed Cop** | | | |
| Los Feliz Hotel | 3101 | Los Feliz Bl | Los Angeles |
| **Framed Cop** | | | |
| Building | 3126 | Los Feliz Bl | Los Angeles |
| **Framed Cop** | | | |
| Building | 4150 | Los Feliz Bl | Los Angeles |
| **Framed Cop** | | | |
| Intersection | | Los Feliz Bl and Perlita Av | Los Angeles |
| **Framed Cop** | | | |
| Intersection | | Los Feliz Bl and San Fernando Rd | Glendale |

| Location | Number | Street | City |
|---|---|---|---|
| **Express Delivery** | | | |
| The Maple Shop | 206 W | Los Feliz Bl | Glendale |
| **Gem Robbery** (Season 4) | | | |
| House | 531 N | Lucerne Bl | Los Angeles |
| **Chain Store** | | | |
| Nursery possibly | 12920 | Magnolia Bl | Sherman Oaks |
| **Phony Cop** | | | |
| Building | 24347 | Main St | Newhall |
| **Reformed Criminal** | | | |
| Building | 24355 | Main St | Newhall |
| **Reformed Criminal** | | | |
| Building | 24359 | Main St | Newhall |
| **Reformed Criminal** | | | |
| Soledad Hotel | 24367 | Main St | Newhall |
| **Reformed Criminal** | | | |
| Paul Palmer, Attorney | 24369 | Main St | Newhall |
| **Reformed Criminal** | | | |
| Cocktail Lounge | 24371 | Main St | Newhall |
| **Reformed Criminal** | | | |
| West side of block | 520 | Main St | El Segundo |
| **Reckless Driving** | | | |
| Building | 520 | Main St | El Segundo |
| **Reckless Driving** | | | |
| Intersection | | March Av and Ingomar St | Canoga Park |
| **Scared Cop** | | | |
| House | 857 N | Martel Av | Los Angeles |
| **Runaway Boy** | | | |
| House | 903 N | Martel Av | Los Angeles |
| **Runaway Boy** | | | |
| House | 104 S | Medio Dr | Los Angeles |
| **Christmas Story** | | | |
| Building | NW corner of | Melrose and Spaulding Av | Los Angeles |
| **Gambling Story** | | | |
| Gene's Auto Works | 7229 | Melrose Av | Los Angeles |
| **Killer on the Run** | | | |
| William C Jagy Service Station | 7253 | Melrose Av | Los Angeles |
| **Killer on the Run** | | | |
| Alley behind | 7308 | Melrose Av | Los Angeles |
| **Dead Patrolman** | | | |
| Nielsen's Books | 7308 | Melrose Av | Los Angeles |
| **Dead Patrolman** | | | |
| Building | 7326 | Melrose Av | Los Angeles |
| **Dead Patrolman** | | | |
| Myrts Corner Hamburger Stand | 7350 | Melrose Av | Los Angeles |
| **Counterfeit** | | | |
| Melrose Market | 7355 | Melrose Av | Los Angeles |
| **Counterfeit** | | | |
| Novelty Quilting | 7373 | Melrose Av | Los Angeles |
| **Dead Patrolman** | | | |
| Building | 7710 | Melrose Av | Los Angeles |
| **Gambling Story** | | | |
| Corner | | Melrose Av and Fuller Av | Los Angeles |
| **Dead Patrolman** | | | |
| Building | NE corner of | Melrose Av and Genesee Av | Los Angeles |
| **Gambling Story** | | | |

| | | Mira Loma Av and Gardena Av | Glendale |
|---|---|---|---|
| House | | | |

**Gem Robbery** (Season 4)

| | | | |
|---|---|---|---|
| Apartments | 14047 | Moorpark St | Sherman Oaks |

**Split Robbery**

| | | | |
|---|---|---|---|
| Park Seville Apartments | 14065 | Moorpark St | Sherman Oaks |

**Expose**

| | | | |
|---|---|---|---|
| Huse | 15341 | Mulholland Dr | Los Angeles |

**Motorcycle** (Season 2)

| | | | |
|---|---|---|---|
| House | 15433 | Mulholland Dr | Los Angeles |

**Magazine Writer**

| | | | |
|---|---|---|---|
| The Overlook | 16471 | Mulholland Dr | Encino |

**Mexican Chase**

| | | | |
|---|---|---|---|
| Mountain Patrol Fire Station 2 | 16500 | Mulholland Dr | Encino |

**Armored Car**
**Copter Cave In**
**Detour to Death**
**Diversion Robbery**
**Double Copter**
**Hired Killer**
**Hostage-Copter**
**Hostage Family Copter**
**Hot Cargo**
**Hypo Bandit**
**Kidnap-Copter**
**Magazine Writer**
**Mexican Chase**
**Migrant Workers**
**Motorcycle** (Season 2)
**Nitro**
**Tear Gas Copter**
**Witness Wife**
**Woman Escapes**

| | | | |
|---|---|---|---|
| Mulholland Dr west of | 16500 | Mulholland Dr | Encino |

**Mexican Chase**
**Oil Lease**

| | | | |
|---|---|---|---|
| Intersection | | Mulholland Dr and Bowmont Dr | Los Angeles |

**Slain Cabby**
**Trojan Horse**

| | | | |
|---|---|---|---|
| House nearest | | Mulholland Dr and Bowmont Dr | Los Angeles |

**Trojan Horse**

| | | | |
|---|---|---|---|
| Intersection | | Mulholland Dr and Encino Hills Dr | Encino |

**Hostage-Copter**

| | | | |
|---|---|---|---|
| Intersection | | Mulholland Dr and Franklin Canyon | Los Angeles |

**Mistaken Identity**

| | | | |
|---|---|---|---|
| Intersection | | Mulholland Dr and Roscomare Rd | Los Angeles |

**Auto Press**

| | | | |
|---|---|---|---|
| Runyon Park | | Mulholland Dr and Runyon Canyon Rd | Los Angeles |

**Officer's Wife**

| | | | |
|---|---|---|---|
| Intersection | | Mulholland Dr and Torreyson Dr | Los Angeles |

**Explosives**
**Killer on the Run**

| | | | |
|---|---|---|---|
| House | 24317 N | Newhall Av | Newhall |
| **Escort** | | | |
| **Girl Bandit** | | | |
| Mayo Motel | 903 (841 N) | New Depot St (Figueroa St [original]) | Los Angeles |
| **Bank Messenger** | | | |
| Traveling shot | | Nichols Canyon | Los Angeles |
| **Explosives** | | | |
| Telephone booth | | Nichols Canyon and Willow Glen | Los Angeles |
| **Killer on the Run** | | | |
| House | 2025 | Nichols Canyon Rd | Los Angeles |
| **Temptation** | | | |
| Stationary shot | 2533 near | Nichols Canyon Rd | Los Angeles |
| **Explosives** | | | |
| Intersection | | Nichols Canyon Rd and Del Zuro Dr | Los Angeles |
| **Dead Patrolman** | | | |
| Intersection | | Nichols Canyon Rd and La Cuesta Dr | Los Angeles |
| **Dead Patrolman** | | | |
| Traveling shot | | Nicholson St towards Culver Bl | Playa del Rey |
| **Radioactive** | | | |
| House | 1541 N | Ogden Dr | Los Angeles |
| **Brave Boy** | | | |
| across from | 1549 N | Ogden Dr | Los Angeles |
| **Brave Boy** | | | |
| House | 1609 N | Ogden Dr | Los Angeles |
| **Brave Boy** | | | |
| House | 1623 N | Ogden Dr | Los Angeles |
| **Brave Boy** | | | |
| House | 1629 N | Ogden Dr | Los Angeles |
| **Brave Boy** | | | |
| Starlite Lodge | 3320 W | Olive Av | Burbank |
| **License Plates** | | | |
| Garages at alley next to | 11643 | Otsego St | Los Angeles |
| **Taxi** | | | |
| Ballona Creek Bridge | | Overland Av | Culver City |
| **Hit and Run** (Season 1) | | | |
| House | 10210 | Owensmouth Av | Chatsworth |
| **Safecracker** | | | |
| Houses | east of Colfax Av | Oxnard St | Los Angeles |
| **Taxi** | | | |
| Paradise Cove and Pier | 28128 | Pacific Coast Hwy | Malibu |
| **Harbor Story** | | | |
| Farm | near Hughes Airport now under water just north of | Palawan Wy | Marina Del Rey |
| **Hit and Run** (Season 1) | | | |
| Library Park | | Palm Av and Richmond St | El Segundo |
| **Lookout** | | | |
| Traveling shot | 12900 block | Panama St | Los Angeles |
| **Hit and Run** (Season 1) | | | |
| House | 12961 | Panama St | Los Angeles |
| **Hit and Run** (Season 1) | | | |
| House | 4301 | Parva Av | Los Angeles |

| | | | |
|---|---|---|---|
| **Double Death** | | | |
| Ranch north of Plummer | | Bothwell Rd Melvin Av Citronia St Ballinger St | Northridge |
| **Fire** | | | |
| Former Bridge crossing | | Plummer St and Hanna Ave | Chatsworth |
| **Mental Patient** | | | |
| House on hill | | Plummer St and Topanga Canyon Pl | Chatsworth |
| **Mental Patient** | | | |
| House | 1233 | Poinsettia Dr | Los Angeles |
| **Convict's Wife** | | | |
| Apartments | | Poinsettia Dr and Hampton Av | Los Angeles |
| **Convict's Wife** | | | |
| House | 1165 | Poinsettia Pl | Los Angeles |
| **Armored Car** | | | |
| CHP Headquarters | 936 N | Poinsettia Pl | Los Angeles |
| **Missing Witness** | | | |
| **Typhoid Carrier** | | | |
| Park | SW corner | Poinsettia Pl and Romaine St | Los Angeles |
| **Cargo Hi Jack** | | | |
| **Runaway Boy** | | | |
| Building | NW corner | Poinsettia Place and Romaine St | Los Angeles |
| **Cargo Hi Jack** | | | |
| Saugus Cafe | 25861 | Railroad Av | Santa Clarita |
| **Girl Bandit** | | | |
| Intersection | | Ranch Rd and Eveward Rd | Culver City |
| **Radioactive** | | | |
| Griffith Park Fern Dell Nature Museum | 5375 | Red Oak Dr | Los Angeles |
| **The Trucker** | | | |
| Mick's Grill | 8322 | Reseda Bl | Northridge |
| **Dan Sick** | | | |
| **Narcotics Racket** | | | |
| Building | 8627 | Reseda Bl | Northridge |
| **Train Copter** | | | |
| Northridge Lumber Co | 8703 | Reseda Bl | Northridge |
| **Fire** | | | |
| Building | 8725 | Reseda Bl | Northridge |
| **Train Copter** | | | |
| Building | 8727 | Reseda Bl | Northridge |
| **Train Copter** | | | |
| Allen's Market | 8738 | Reseda Bl | Northridge |
| **Fire** | | | |
| Building | 8814 | Reseda Bl | Northridge |
| **Narcotics Racket** | | | |
| Walter D. Bigg Jeweler | 8827 | Reseda Bl | Northridge |
| **Narcotics Racket** | | | |
| Bernard Grossman Attorney at Law | 8829 | Reseda Bl | Northridge |
| **Confession** | | | |
| Realty Office | 8830 | Reseda Bl | Northridge |
| **Confession** | | | |
| Johnny's Shoe Service | 8831 | Reseda Bl | Northridge |
| **Confession** | | | |
| Medical building | 8833 | Reseda Bl | Northridge |
| **Confession** | | | |

| | | | |
|---|---|---|---|
| The Liquor House | 8834 | Reseda Bl | Northridge |
| **Confession** | | | |
| Building | 8883 | Reseda Bl | Northridge |
| **Confession** | | | |
| Building | 8900 | Reseda Bl | Northridge |
| **Confession** | | | |
| SP Northridge Train Station | | Reseda Bl and Parthenia Pl | Northridge |
| **Fire** | | | |
| **Train Copter** | | | |
| Bill's Market | 20059 | Roscoe Bl | Winnetka |
| **Hot Rod** | | | |
| Building | 20851 | Roscoe Bl | Winnetka |
| **Hot Rod** | | | |
| Curragh Stock Farm | 22901 | Roscoe Bl (NW of Fallbrook Av and Eccles St) | Canoga Park |
| **Typhoid Carrier** | | | |
| Busch Brewery | | Roscoe Bl and Haskell Av | Van Nuys |
| **Motel Robbery** | | | |
| House | 3465 | Rowena Av | Los Angeles |
| **Framed Cop** | | | |
| House | 3472 | Rowena Av | Los Angeles |
| **Framed Cop** | | | |
| Pedestrian Undercrossing | | Sale Av and Del Valle St | Woodland Hills |
| **The Trap** | | | |
| 4 chimneys near intersection | S | San Fernando Rd and Sheldon St | Los Angeles |
| **Efficiency Secretary** | | | |
| Bank | 1148 | San Fernando Rd | San Fernando |
| **Machine-Napping** | | | |
| Crossing street | 1201 | San Fernando Rd | San Fernando |
| **Machine-Napping** | | | |
| Helms Pontiac-Cadillac | 1212 | San Fernando Rd | San Fernando |
| **Machine-Napping** | | | |
| Mayfair Market | 1320 | San Fernando Rd | San Fernando |
| **Escort** | | | |
| SP Taylor Yard | Rio de Los Angeles State Park next to | San Fernando Rd | Los Angeles |
| **Blood Money** | | | |
| Underpass | | San Fernando Rd and Golden State Fwy | Los Angeles |
| **Escort** | | | |
| Bank of America | | San Fernando Rd and W. Cerritos Av | Glendale |
| **Express Delivery** | | | |
| **Gem Robbery** (Season 4) | | | |
| Traveling shot | 638 | San Fernando Rd at Ilex St | San Fernando |
| **Escort** | | | |
| California Bank | 11944 | San Vicente Bl | Los Angeles |
| **Stolen Car Ring** | | | |
| Alley between | 11975 and 11969 | San Vicente Bl | Los Angeles |
| **Stolen Car Ring** | | | |
| Corner | | San Vicente Bl and La | Los Angeles |

496

| | | | |
|---|---|---|---|
| **Stolen Car Ring** | | | |
| Apartment | 10460 | Santa Monica Bl | Los Angeles |
| **Portrait of Death** | | | |
| Mormon Temple | 10777 | Santa Monica  Bl | Los Angeles |
| **Stolen Car Ring** | | | |
| Pacific Electric Sherman Yard | 8800 | Santa Monica Bl | West L. A. |
| **Hit and Run** (Season 3) | | | |
| **Temptation** | | | |
| Travelodge | 10740 | Santa Monica Bl | Los Angeles |
| **Stolen Car Ring** | | | |
| Hal Jaffe Auto Repair | 7601 | Santa Monica Bl | Los Angeles |
| **Brave Boy** | | | |
| Ervin's Auto Wrecking | 8775 | Santa Monica Bl | West L. A. |
| **Plant Robbery** | | | |
| Kay & Art's Cafe | 8785 | Santa Monica Bl | West L. A. |
| **Plant Robbery** | | | |
| California Super Service (Gas Station) | 8797 | Santa Monica Bl | West L. A. |
| **Plant Robbery** | | | |
| Shermart Market Grocery | 8840 | Santa Monica Bl | West L. A. |
| **Armored Car** | | | |
| **Plant Robbery** | | | |
| Building | 8841 | Santa Monica Bl | West L. A. |
| **Armored Car** | | | |
| Hotel | 8869 | Santa Monica Bl | West L.A. |
| **Armored Car** | | | |
| Paul's Radio Service | 8870 | Santa Monica Bl | West L. A. |
| **Armored Car** | | | |
| alley north of | | Santa Monica Bl between Spaulding Av and Curson Av | Los Angeles |
| | | | |
| **Brave Boy** | | | |
| Iverson Movie Ranch | | Santa Susana Pass Rd | Chatsworth |
| **Plane Crash** | | | |
| Monahan's Inn | 16848 | Saticoy St | Van Nuys |
| **Hot Rod** | | | |
| Verdugo Escrow | 17319 | Saticoy St | Van Nuys |
| **Safecracker** | | | |
| **Trailer Story** | | | |
| Guy's Sporting Goods | 17321 | Saticoy St | Van Nuys |
| **Safecracker** | | | |
| **Trailer Story** | | | |
| Greene Jewelers and Gift Wear | 17322 | Saticoy St | Van Nuys |
| **Safecracker** | | | |
| **Trailer Story** | | | |
| Multiple angles | | Saticoy St and Gaynor Av | Van Nuys |
| | | | |
| **Motel Robbery** | | | |
| House (front and rear) | 814 N | Screenland Dr | Burbank |
| **License Plates** | | | |
| House (all south to corner) | 815 N | Screenland Dr | Burbank |
| **License Plates** | | | |
| House | 819 N | Screenland Dr | Burbank |
| **License Plates** | | | |
| House | 823 N | Screenland Dr | Burbank |
| **License Plates** | | | |
| SW corner | | Screenland Dr and Clark Ave | Burbank |
| | | | |
| **License Plates** | | | |

| | | | |
|---|---|---|---|
| NE corner | | Screenland Dr and Clark Ave | Burbank |
| **License Plates** | | | |
| Alley from | | Screenland Dr to N Hollywood Wy | Burbank |
| **License Plates** | | | |
| Intersection | | Selma Av and Courtney Av | Los Angeles |
| **Brave Boy** | | | |
| Intersection | | Selma Av and Ogden Dr | Los Angeles |
| **Brave Boy** | | | |
| Barn site approximately where | | Semrad Rd would cross Bell Creek between Highlander Rd and Hartland St | West Hills (Castle Peak in background) |
| **Stripped Cars** | | | |
| Real Estate | 7246 | Sepulveda Bl | Van Nuys |
| **Lie Detector** | | | |
| Deeks Realty | 7500 | Sepulveda Bl | Van Nuys |
| **Lie Detector** | | | |
| San Fernando Valley Motel | 7533 | Sepulveda Bl | Van Nuys |
| **Lie Detector** | | | |
| Monticello Hotel | 8071 | Sepulveda Bl | Van Nuys |
| **Motel Robbery** | | | |
| Panorama Motel | 8209 | Sepulveda Bl | Van Nuys |
| **Motel Robbery** | | | |
| Rita Curtis Swim School | 8220 | Sepulveda Bl | Van Nuys |
| **Motel Robbery** | | | |
| Pacific Lodge Youth Services | 4900 | Serrania Av | Woodland Hills |
| **Gambling** | | | |
| prob North Hollywood Concrete Tile Co | 12323 | Sherman Wy | North Hollywood |
| **The Search** | | | |
| CHP Headquarters (rear) | 18238 | Sherman Wy | Reseda |
| **Statute of Limitations** | | | |
| McMahan Furniture Store | 18344 | Sherman Wy | Reseda |
| **Statute of Limitations** | | | |
| Lawson Jewelers | 18353 | Sherman Wy | Reseda |
| **Phony Insurance** | | | |
| Anita | 18361 | Sherman Wy | Reseda |
| **Phony Insurance** | | | |
| **Statute of Limitations** | | | |
| Joe Hran Texaco SE corner | | Sierra Hwy and Soledad Canyon Rd | Santa Clarita |
| **Girl Bandit** | | | |
| **Reformed Criminal** | | | |
| Log Cabin Motel next to Joe Hran's Texaco SE corner | | Sierra Hwy and Soledad Canyon Rd | Santa Clarita |
| **Girl Bandit** | | | |
| Saugus Speedway | 22500 | Soledad Canyon Rd | Saugus |
| **Girl Bandit** | | | |
| Young Israel | 660 N | Spaulding Av | Los Angeles |
| **Killer on the Run** | | | |
| Stone Printing Co | 681 | Spaulding Av | Los Angeles |
| **Killer on the Run** | | | |
| House | 740 N | Spaulding Av | Los Angeles |
| **Gambling Story** | | | |
| Old Lodge | | Stadium Wy | Los Angeles |
| **Foster Child** | | | |

| Location | Number | Street | City |
|---|---|---|---|
| Barlow Hospital | 2000 | Stadium Wy | Los Angeles |
| **Family Affair** | | | |
| Fwy Underpass | | Stadium Wy | Los Angeles |
| **Bank Messenger** | | | |
| Intersection | | Stadium Wy and Boylston St | Los Angeles |
| **Blood Money** | | | |
| **False Confession** | | | |
| House | 4101 | Stansbury Av | Sherman Oaks |
| **Double Cross** | | | |
| Traveling shot | | Stansbury Av and Roblar Rd | Sherman Oaks |
| **Double Cross** | | | |
| Hilltop house | above int | Summitridge Dr and Beverly Park St | Beverly Hills |
| **Ranch-Copter** | | | |
| **Tear Gas Copter** | | | |
| **Witness Wife** | | | |
| East from Medio Dr | | Sunset Bl | Los Angeles |
| **Christmas Story** | | | |
| Gas Station | 1106 | Sunset Bl | Los Angeles |
| **False Confession** | | | |
| Paradise Motel | 1116 | Sunset Bl | Los Angeles |
| **False Confession** | | | |
| Brentwood Motor Hotel | 12200 W | Sunset Bl | Los Angeles |
| **Christmas Story** | | | |
| Harrington Motel | 5224 | Sunset Bl | Los Angeles |
| **Rabies** | | | |
| TraveLodge | 7370 | Sunset Bl | Los Angeles |
| **Killer on the Run** | | | |
| House | 7758 | Sunset Bl | Los Angeles |
| **Brave Boy** | | | |
| Building | 7801 | Sunset Bl | Los Angeles |
| **Temptation** | | | |
| Sunset Tower Hotel | 9358 | Sunset Bl | West L. A. |
| **Hit and Run** (Season 3) | | | |
| **Temptation** | | | |
| Gas Station | 116 | Sunset Bl | Los Angeles |
| **False Confession** | | | |
| Business | 4529 | Sylmar Av | Sherman Oaks |
| **Diversion Robbery** | | | |
| Sylmar Palms Apartments | 4555 | Sylmar Av | Sherman Oaks |
| **Diversion Robbery** | | | |
| Between | | Tampa Av and Vanalden Av north of Plummer St | Northridge |
| **Confession** | | | |
| North towards Parthenia St | | Topanga Canyon Bl | Chatsworth |
| **Hitchhiker** | | | |
| South towards Plummer St | | Topanga Canyon Bl | Chatsworth |
| **Hitchhiker** | | | |
| Chatsworth Community Church | 10051 | Topanga Canyon Bl | Chatsworth |
| **Safecracker** | | | |
| Gas Station | 10124 | Topanga Canyon Bl | Chatsworth |
| **Ex Con** | | | |
| **Fake Cop** | | | |
| **Resident Officer** | | | |
| Chatsworth Market | 10249 | Topanga Canyon Bl | Chatsworth |
| **Motorcycle** (Season 1) | | | |

| Location | | Number | Street | City |
| --- | --- | --- | --- | --- |
| Town & Country Cafe | | 10255 | Topanga Canyon Bl | Chatsworth |
| **Motorcycle** (Season 1) | | | | |
| **Safecracker** | | | | |
| The Wooden Shoe | | 8240 | Topanga Canyon Bl | Canoga Park |
| **Typhoid Carrier** | | | | |
| Chatsworth Lumber | | 9754 | Topanga Canyon Bl | Chatsworth |
| **Motorcycle** (Season 1) | | | | |
| Intersection | | | Topanga Canyon Bl and Andora Av | Chatsworth |
| **Fake Cop** | | | | |
| Building | | NW corner of | Topanga Canyon Bl and Avenue San Luis | Woodland Hills |
| **Anti-Toxin** | | | | |
| Intersection | | | Topanga Canyon Bl and Marilla St | Chatsworth |
| **Motorcycle** (Season 1) | | | | |
| Street view | | | Topanga Canyon Bl north of Church | Chatsworth |
| **Safecracker** | | | | |
| West of T.P.Blvd | | | Tulsa St | Chatsworth |
| **Female Hitchhiker** | | | | |
| **Resident Officer** | | | | |
| near | | 23236 | Valley Circle Bl | Chatsworth |
| **Ex Con** | | | | |
| Chatsworth Reservoir | | | Valley Circle Bl west of Plummer St | Chatsworth |
| **Mental Patient** | | | | |
| next to Weddington Golf | | | Valley Spring Ln | Studio City |
| **Split Robbery** | | | | |
| Telephone booth | | SE corner | Valley Spring Ln and Bellaire Ave | Studio City |
| **Split Robbery** | | | | |
| House on north side of street between Goodland Av and Valley Spring Ln | | | Valleyheart Dr | Studio City |
| **Split Robbery** | | | | |
| House on north side of street between Alcove Av and Goodland Av | | | Valleyheart Dr | Studio City |
| **Split Robbery** | | | | |
| The Norman Larson Company | | | Van Nuys Airport | Van Nuys |
| **Trailer Story** | | | | |
| Nahas Department Store | | 4520 | Van Nuys Bl | Sherman Oaks |
| **Diversion Robbery** | | | | |
| Sherman Oaks Vacuums | | 4529 | Van Nuys Bl | Encino |
| **Woman Escapes** | | | | |
| Erma May Robbins Cosmetics | | 4531 | Van Nuys Bl | Encino |
| **Woman Escapes** | | | | |
| Joe Ole's Hardware | | 4543 | Van Nuys Bl | Encino |
| **Woman Escapes** | | | | |
| Building | | 4645 | Van Nuys Bl | Sherman Oaks |
| **Expose** | | | | |
| CHP Headquarters | | 5539 | Van Nuys Bl | Sherman Oaks |
| **Expose** | | | | |
| House | | 9839 | Vanalden Av | Northridge |
| **Confession** | | | | |
| House | | 9857 | Vanalden Ave | Northridge |
| **Dan Sick** | | | | |
| **Hot Rod** | | | | |
| Intersection | | | Vanalden Av and Kinzie St | Northridge |

| | | | |
|---|---|---|---|
| **Confession** | | | |
| Intersection | | Vanalden Av and Marilla St | Northridge |
| **Narcotics Racket** | | | |
| Behind | 13629 | Ventura Bl | Sherman Oaks |
| **Human Bomb** | | | |
| Tropi Kool Pools | 13865 | Ventura Bl | Sherman Oaks |
| **Double Cross** | | | |
| Behind | 13900 | Ventura Bl | Sherman Oaks |
| **Double Cross** | | | |
| Escrow Guarantee | 13900 | Ventura Bl | Sherman Oaks |
| **Double Cross** | | | |
| Rand's Ventura Round-Up | 13920 | Ventura Bl | Sherman Oaks |
| **Mistaken Identity** | | | |
| Steele's Motor Lodge | 13949 | Ventura Bl | Sherman Oaks |
| **Split Robbery** | | | |
| Ralphs | 14049 | Ventura Bl | Sherman Oaks |
| **Split Robbery** | | | |
| Building | 14060 | Ventura Bl | Sherman Oaks |
| **Split Robbery** | | | |
| Sherman Oaks Jewelers | 14522 | Ventura Bl | Sherman Oaks |
| **Diversion Robbery** | | | |
| Victory Motel | 15052 | Ventura Bl | Los Angeles |
| **Deadly Diamonds** | | | |
| Travelodge | 16117 | Ventura Bl | Encino |
| **Resort** | | | |
| Huckins Steaks | 17301 | Ventura Bl | Encino |
| **Narcotics Racket** | | | |
| Encino Oaks Motor Lodge | 17323 | Ventura Bl | Encino |
| **Narcotics Racket** | | | |
| A & B Motors | 19326 | Ventura Bl | Los Angeles |
| **Hitchhiker** | | | |
| Neider's Body Shop | 22440 | Ventura Bl | Woodland Hills |
| **The Trap** | | | |
| Woodland Hills Pet Shop | 22543 | Ventura Bl | Woodland Hills |
| **The Trap** | | | |
| Lee's Steak House Hideaway Room | 22611 | Ventura Bl | Woodland Hills |
| **The Trap** | | | |
| Merrill's Feed & Saddlery | 22705 | Ventura Bl | Woodland Hills |
| **The Trap** | | | |
| William R. Wilson Jr. Insurance | 22708 | Ventura Bl | Woodland Hills |
| **The Trap** | | | |
| Wishing Well Cafe | 22941 | Ventura Bl | Los Angeles |
| **Released Convict** | | | |
| Golden Pheasant Restaurant/Billingsley Steak House | 26300 | Ventura Bl | Calabasas |
| **Road-Block** | | | |
| Motel next to | 26300 | Ventura Bl | Calabasas |
| **Frightened Witness** | | | |
| Stationary shot | E of 101 fwy exit | Ventura Bl | Woodland Hills |
| **The Trap** | | | |
| Traveling shot | | Ventura Bl and Alhama Dr | Woodland Hills |
| **Gambling** | | | |
| Building | SE corner of | Ventura Bl and Coldwater Canyon Av | Studio City |
| **Split Robbery** | | | |
| Maple Leaf Motel | 13901 | Ventura Bl | Sherman Oaks |
| **Double Cross** | | | |

**Expose**
**Mistaken Identity**

| Location | Number | Street | City |
|---|---|---|---|
| Apartments | 4321 | Ventura Canyon Av | Sherman Oaks |

**Human Bomb**

| Location | Number | Street | City |
|---|---|---|---|
| Eugene's Jewelers | 1745 N | Vermont Av | Los Angeles |

**Hypo Bandit**

| Location | Number | Street | City |
|---|---|---|---|
| House | 2535 N | Vermont Av | Los Angeles |

**Suspected Cop**

| Location | Number | Street | City |
|---|---|---|---|
| Griffith Park Vermont Av entrance | 2700 N | Vermont Av | Los Angeles |

**Hypo Bandit**

| Location | Number | Street | City |
|---|---|---|---|
| North of Greek Theater | N | Vermont Av | Los Angeles |

**Suspected Cop**

| Location | Number | Street | City |
|---|---|---|---|
| Griffith Park Tunnel | N | Vermont Canyon Rd | Los Angeles |

**Machine-Napping**

| Location | Number | Street | City |
|---|---|---|---|
| House | 12764 | Victory Bl | Burbank |

**Slain Cabby**

| Location | Number | Street | City |
|---|---|---|---|
| Knoll Crest Realty | 12800 | Victory Bl | Burbank |

**Trailer Story**

| Location | Number | Street | City |
|---|---|---|---|
| Gas Station | 1200 N | Virgil Av | Los Angeles |

**Convicted Innocent**
**Double Death**

| Location | Number | Street | City |
|---|---|---|---|
| House | 1215 N | Virgil Av | Los Angeles |

**Convicted Innocent**

| Location | Number | Street | City |
|---|---|---|---|
| Sand Dune Smoke Stack | | Vista del Mar | El Segundo |

**Reckless Driving**

| Location | Number | Street | City |
|---|---|---|---|
| near | 608 | Washington Bl | Los Angeles |

**Car Theft**

| Location | Number | Street | City |
|---|---|---|---|
| Intersection | | Weddington St and Bakman Av | Los Angeles |

**Taxi**

| Location | Number | Street | City |
|---|---|---|---|
| House | 628 N | Westbourne Dr | West L.A. |

**Hit and Run** (Season 3)

| Location | Number | Street | City |
|---|---|---|---|
| Lehrer Fine Furs | 1167 N | Western Av | Los Angeles |

**Hypo Bandit**

| Location | Number | Street | City |
|---|---|---|---|
| Andrews Window Shade & Floor Covering Co | 1175 N | Western Av | Los Angeles |

**Hypo Bandit**

| Location | Number | Street | City |
|---|---|---|---|
| Whiteman Airport | | Whiteman Airport | Pacoima |

**Efficiency Secretary**
**Stolen Plane-Copter**

NE Whiteman towards Hansen Dam

**Efficiency Secretary**

| Location | Number | Street | City |
|---|---|---|---|
| American Lutheran Church | 755 N | Whitnall Hwy | Burbank |

**License Plates**

| Location | Number | Street | City |
|---|---|---|---|
| Hollywood Police Station | 1358 | Wilcox Av | Los Angeles |

**License Plates**

| Location | Number | Street | City |
|---|---|---|---|
| SW corner of alley west of Highland Av | | Willoughby Av | Los Angeles |

**Counterfeit**
**Girl Bandit**

| Location | Number | Street | City |
|---|---|---|---|
| Apartments | 6815 | Willoughby Av | Los Angeles |

**Counterfeit**

| Location | Number | Street | City |
|---|---|---|---|
| Apartments | 6851 | Willoughby Av | Los Angeles |

**Counterfeit**

| Location | Number | Street | City |
|---|---|---|---|
| Apartments | 7416 | Willoughby Av | Los Angeles |

**Runaway Boy**

| Location | Number | Street | City |
|---|---|---|---|
| NE corner alley west of Highland Av | | Willoughby Av | |

**Girl Bandit**

| Location | Number | Street | City |
|---|---|---|---|
| Alley south of Bekins | | Romaine St to Willoughby Av between | Los Angeles |

| | | Highland Av and Citrus Av | |
|---|---|---|---|
| **Counterfeit**<br>Intersection | | Willow Glen Rd and Harlesden Ct | Los Angeles |
| **Killer on the Run**<br>Intersection | | Willow Glen Rd and Woodstock Rd | Los Angeles |
| **Killer on the Run**<br>Intersection | | Willow Glen Rd and Zorada Dr | Los Angeles |
| **Temptation**<br>Frank's Nurseries | 12424 | Wilshire Bl | Los Angeles |
| **Stolen Car Ring**<br>Douglas Park | | Wilshire Bl and Chelsea Av | Los Angeles |
| **Stolen Car Ring**<br>Chuck's Fountain & Grill | 8257 | Winnetka Av | Canoga Park |
| **Hot Rod**<br>Intersection | | Woodlake Av and Justice St | Canoga Park |
| **Scared Cop**<br>Traveling shot | possibly near | Woodlake Av and Strathern St | Canoga Park |
| **Scared Cop**<br>Nifty Food Market | 4742 | Woodman Av | Sherman Oaks |
| **Slain Cabby**<br>From Dumetz Rd | | Ybarra Rd | Woodland Hills |
| **Released Convict** | | | |

# ZIV STUDIO AND BACKLOT

ZIV Studio Backlot
- **Bank Messenger**
- **Careless Cop**
- **Cargo Hi Jack**
- **Convict's Wife**
- **Credit Card**
- **Desperate Men**
- **Explosives**
- **Fear**
- **Fisherman's Luck**
- **Frightened Witness**
- **Gem Robbery** (Season 2)
- **Hitchhiker**
- **Hitchhiker Dies**
- **Hot Dust**
- **Illegal Entry**
- **The Judge**
- **Lady Bandits**
- **Machine-Napping**
- **Motorcycle** (Season 1)
- **Plant Robbery**
- **Prospector**
- **Runaway Boy**
- **Scared Cop**
- **Slain Cabby**
- **Stolen Car Ring**
- **Trojan Horse**

**The Trucker**
**Typhoid Carrier**

# VENTURA COUNTY

| 279 | Towing Garage | 4456 | Los Angeles Av | Simi Valley |
|---|---|---|---|---|
| | **Train Robbery** | | | |
| 280 | SP Simi Valley Train Station, near | 4465 | Los Angeles Av | Simi Valley |
| | **Train Robbery** | | | |
| 115 | Back road | | Conejo Valley Airport | Thousand Oaks |
| | **Retied Gangster** | | | |
| 117 | House | 2884 | Crescent Wy | Thousand Oaks |
| | **Father Thief** | | | |
| 207 | Janss Ranch House/Cameron Center | 288 | Greenmeadow Dr | Thousand Oaks |
| | **Retired Gangster** | | | |
| 301 | Ranch on hill | | Marin St | Thousand Oaks |
| | **Desert Town** | | | |
| 470 | Behind | 2860 E | Thousand Oaks Bl | Thousand Oaks |
| | **Father Thief** | | | |
| 471 | Building | 2974 E | Thousand Oaks Bl | Thousand Oaks |
| | **Father Thief** | | | |
| 472 | Max & Rose Cafe | 3006 E | Thousand Oaks Bl | Thousand Oaks |
| | **Father Thief** | | | |
| 473 | Junior Department Store | 3021 E | Thousand Oaks Bl | Thousand Oaks |
| | **Father Thief** | | | |
| 474 | Conejo Pharmacy | 3041 E | Thousand Oaks Bl | Thousand Oaks |
| | **Father Thief** | | | |